Cotton Candy
and Carrousels
The World of Special Children

Cotton Candy
and Carrousels
The World of Special Children

by Margaret Humphries Callihan

The Naylor Company
Book Publishers of the Southwest
San Antonio, Texas

Library of Congress Cataloging in Publication Data
Callihan, Margaret Humphries, 1930-
  Cotton candy and carrousels.

  1. Mentally handicapped children — Education.
I. Title.
LC4601.C26   371.9′28   72-6139
ISBN 0-8111-0464-8

Preface

The people in this story are real, children and adults. The diagrams included are those I used in the classroom with them. The reproductions of the students' work are duplicates of the work they turned in to me in class. None was done at home. The ages of these children varied between eleven and sixteen, chronologically. Mentally they were much, much younger. I do not care to quote statistics nor the I.Q. level. For a child to be in an Opportunity School such as ours, he had to be below the so-called "dull-normal." Some achieved first grade work . . . each tried, each worked, each improved . . . especially I, their teacher.

Margaret Humphries Callihan

Contents

Cotton Candy

Nudging, pushing, counting skinny pennies
Children watch the mounds of soft-spun pink.
A father's head shows here and there like thistle
In a violet bed. A voice, half-frightened, asks
"How much for one?"
  "Two nickels, Boy, that's all."
The voice from counter-level stops, then pipes up
Loud and clear,
  "Does you sell halfs, Mister?"

I I WAS SITTING behind a desk, as were several other teachers, waiting for the students and their parents to come for registration. I was particularly excited, more so than the students, I think, for this was my first experience in the Opportunity School. After three years in high school, teaching Spanish and English, I had at last come into the field in which I was most interested.

This then is my story. I shall not quote statistics or theory. This is but a personal account of the year I spent teaching mentally retarded children — my year as an unwed mother of sixteen little people. It was a beautiful exper-

1

ience that I shall cherish always. At the time I began my year with the children I did not know, of course, that the following fall I would marry and move to another city. Thus my stay with them was a very brief nine months.

The children began to come into the room. Most of them were accompanied by their parents, for only a few were capable of giving all of the information necessary to register. I asked questions and filled in blanks for several hours, all the while noticing how quiet the children were. They sat or stood close to their parents and, for the most part, did not talk. They were simply there — staring at me. Each time I looked up from my desk I met a pair of incredulous eyes. Something was the matter. I had not the slightest idea what it could be, but I felt uneasy. Finally a cute, little, blond-headed boy came to my rescue. When his mother stood up to leave, she turned to her son and said, "Nicky, this is your new teacher."

Nicky came around behind the desk and gave me a big hug. "I like you. You're pretty," he said.

"And I like you, Nicky. I'm so glad that you are going to be in my room." He smiled, hugged me again, and left.

Nicky, my little, blond angel, had given me the answer, although I did not realize it at the time. I was a stranger in a new world. I would be accepted eagerly, but it was my job to make the first gesture of friendship, of love. Nicky, unlike the other children, was not content to wait for me.

I cannot possibly describe the step I had taken. For three years I had lectured on American Literature, radical Spanish verbs, and English grammar. I had spoon-fed slow learners and gone to battle with football boys over the merit of turning in assignments on Monday mornings. I had sanctioned; I had chastised. I had preached, wailed, passed, and failed. I had even conquered a rather muscular delinquent and cajoled him into passing English. I had made friends. My teaching was based upon a code in which I firmly

2

believe — treat them as adults whenever possible, be fair, help them if you can. There was room for friendship and undertanding. There was no mention of love and affection. Now I was to lay aside my creed, and most of my three years' experience, and begin a new life, with a new attitude, in a new world.

I shall always remember my first day at school. The children came quietly into my room, sat down at their desks, and began to talk with each other. They were heartily glad to be back at school. As each one entered the room, there was a little cry of delight.

"Oh, Sarah. It's Sarah," and so on. They were greeting old friends from the previous year. I was surprised as I listened to their conversations. They were busily telling each other what had happened during the summer, where they had been, and what they had seen. They talked together as you and I might talk. Some had speech defects, but that was of little consequence. They, too, had news and proceeded to tell it with enthusiasm.

Most of the parents brought their children upstairs and into the room. Then they left. I was surprised that I saw only a few pair of misty eyes. I was sitting at my desk thinking how well things were going when I heard a wail from outside of my door. It was a very loud and unhappy wail. I went into the hall to investigate. There, behind the door, stood a cute little boy with light brown curls and beautiful, blue eyes. At least I thought they were blue, but he was crying so hard that it was difficult to tell. He was not clinging to his mother. He was simply implanted behind the door and was not to be moved. New teacher, that was my first guess, and I was right.

I peeped at Richy and Richy peeped at me. It was a stalemate. I tried to talk with him. I called off the names of some of the children inside. My efforts were fruitless. Richy inundated the hall with tears. Finally I felt so sorry for him that I unthinkingly tried Nicky's trick. I leaned

3

down and hugged him. The tears stopped. I hugged him again and returned to the room. A few minutes later Richy came in. He too was greeted. "It's Richy. Look who's here. Richy!"

A big grin came on Richy's face, and he took his place at a desk. I had the answer to his problem, but it was by no means gone. The first three days of school Richy cried behind the door in the hall; and the first three days I hugged Richy. The fourth day he walked into the room, said good morning, and took his place. I was at last a part of his world. I loved Richy. He felt this — not thought — but felt, and with the feeling came security. Now we belonged together.

I needed a get-acquainted program for the first of school. Knowing this, I made a toy microphone and took it with me. When all of the children were present, I began the day's work.

"How many of you listen to the radio?" Three or four hands went up.

"Such a few? Don't you listen, Sarah?"

"T.V. I like that better." They all agreed and began to talk at once about T.V., the Lone Ranger, and several of their favorite programs. One child volunteered to do a dance she had seen only the night before. The children watched with delight and clapped when the dance was over.

At this point I realized that my orderly little group could probably be heard in the next building, the home of our principal. I stirred myself and quieted the class down.

"We're going to play radio. This is a microphone." Here Felipe told me that you had to talk into it. "You are going to come up as I call your name and tell me who you are, where you live, and what you like to do after school."

Thus the program was under way, or so I thought. Some of the children knew their addresses, even their street numbers. Some did not. Each took the microphone, stood in front of the class, and spoke for a few seconds only. Even Sarah and Nicky who had chattered away earlier were very quiet. After four or five children had taken their turn, I knew that something was wrong. The next child was Richy. I kept him by my side at the desk with my arm around his shoulders. He was cooperation personified. He told me his name, how he liked to play ball after school, and began to talk about his older brother and the children in the neighborhood. He was a good contestant, almost too good. I finally succeeded in getting him back to his seat. After that I had the children stand close by me at the desk. Our closeness gave them confidence and they chattered away. "Radio" was a grand success.

At eleven o'clock that morning we formed a line, walked to the rest rooms, then over to the cafeteria. The children stood in line, took trays and silverware, and selected their lunch. Some paid for it themselves; some had given me their money. Having selected their lunch, they took their places at desks in the auditorium which adjoined the kitchen and served as dining room, auditorium, and theatre. The children ate quietly and chatted with each other and with children from the other rooms.

As soon as I had finished my lunch, I was besieged with "Can I take your tray, Teacher?" I learned that "helping teacher" was considered an honor, one that was to be shared equally, if I were to spare tender feelings.

The children carried their trays to a garbage can, scraped them clean, stacked them neatly on a table, and got in line to return to their room. I was completely amazed. I followed after them in puppy-dog fashion, for certainly they knew more about their school than I did.

We washed again after lunch, as there were several very messy faces, and returned to our room. It was time to rest. The children put their heads on their desks and closed their eyes. Some of them dozed off right away. It was eleven forty-five. They had been at school since eight-thirty

5

and they were tired. This was my first indication as to how easily these children tire.

After our rest period, which lasted about twenty minutes, we went outside to play. I suggested The Farmer in the Dell. I was still trying to match names with faces and this would help me. My idea was at once adopted. After our game the children played on the Jungle Jim, took turns in the swings, and played tag. We stayed outside in the sunshine for half an hour. As I sat on a bench and watched my flock, I thought how very like other children they were. Running, playing, shouting — happy little Indians all. I did not realize at the time that even happy little Indians have problems, and my little Indians were a very special tribe.

When play period was over, we washed and rested again. This time I was glad to rest with them. Afterward I read stories and we had a discussion about the different characters. The children formed a line and we all went downstairs to wait in the hall for their parents. It was two o'clock and school was out. My first day at the Opportunity School was over.

Driving home I noticed that I was tired, but I felt good. Deep down inside I felt very good, and warm, and tender. That night at dinner my family asked me how I liked the children. I could only say, "They're the most affectionate children I've ever known." I could not explain to an outsider the gentle warmth of a smile, the tug on my sleeve of a grimy little hand, nor the honest embrace of a child from another world, my world and theirs. It is a wonderful world of emotion, of make-believe, of trust, and tears, and warmth. It is a world of slow thought and deep feeling, but a happy world of cotton candy and carrousels.

6

II SOON AFTER SCHOOL began, I started to realize how fortunate I was to have the particular group with which I was to work all year. Indeed, I was very fortunate. In the first place most of the children had been together in school for several years. They were accustomed to routine. Getting adjusted to a new teacher would take a little time, but their routine would be uninterrupted.

Secondly, their parents had become adjusted, in varying degrees, to the fact that these children were mentally retarded. Hence the children were sent to school with an attitude of cooperation rather than competition. This was not a school in which Mary or Sam was to outdo his classmates. Rather it was a place in which the child was to achieve his capacity for learning and training, a place in which to adjust to society. This is not to say that competition and recognition were missing. Certainly these factors played an important part in our classroom activities; but each child was recognized and praised according to his individual potential. The feeling of being important is a fundamental necessity to every child regardless of his IQ. It is a part of human nature, and certainly it is paramount to the retarded child.

Another important advantage I had with this group was their educability. These children were capable of learning; and since I was accustomed to teaching, this was to be a great help. I could make actual lesson plans, use books, and even have a form of study period. All of this I was used to so that, even though I had to make a big adjustment in the level of work, I could still use some of the training I had gained in secondary education.

A few months after I first began teaching in high school, I realized that the teacher learns more than the students, particularly in the ways of human nature. By the end of my first year I knew that I had begun to learn an invaluable lesson, patience. I was not a patient person by nature, but at the culmination of my first year I felt that I had made progress. At the end of three years I was still progressing. I had learned not only to be patient but also I had learned the value of being patient with slow learners, of repeating and rephrasing questions, of giving special attention where it was needed. I knew that I could help my students and I knew how to help them. I must say though that during my first few weeks at the Opportunity School I was thrown off balance on many occasions. Several times I questioned the wisdom of having undertaken this new job. Then Nicky or Richy would tug at my hand and smile. "Look, Teacher, what I've done" — a brown and white pony, or a green parrot instead of a purple one. We had progressed a step and I had to stay. I wanted to.

In high school I was accustomed to repeating questions two or three times, usually to different students. Now I found myself asking the same question four or five times, and more often than not, to the same little boy or girl. For a time I had the tendency to pull information from the child. Gradually I learned to distinguish shyness from lack of knowledge. This made my task much easier.

Then I began to develop the prize possession of every teacher — tricks of the trade. Some children are eager to answer questions; others are reticent; some have to be tricked into it. I found that in many cases my children knew an answer but would not reply simply because they had not been coaxed into doing so. In such cases my teaching tricks came into our work.

"Felipe, how much are three and five?"

"Three and five, Teacher?" There was a long pause. Felipe frowned then said he did not know.

"That's all right, Felipe. Now would you come to my desk and count three of these spools and put them to one side?"

Felipe did this easily. Next I had him count five of the spools. Then I asked him to count all of the spools that he had used. He counted out loud to eight. We then decided that three and five are eight. Felipe was very happy. He had given the right answer.

Abstract numbers were difficult. When they came alive as spools or objects in the room to be touched and moved about, the children did much better work. I learned that some of the children who could not do work in their number books could add by going to the board and pointing to large figures that I had drawn for them. One of their favorite lessons was "Copy, count, and color." I put groups of trees, balloons, and so forth on the board. The children counted the figures, drew and colored them on their papers, and wrote the correct number below each group. (Figure 1)

This simple exercise proved far more valuable than I had anticipated. Not only did the children learn to count, but they also learned about colors. I found quite a few of them turning in pages from their coloring books with grass colored purple, cows orange, and people red. Gradually, as we counted and colored, the papers and pictures became more realistic. A few of the children had to learn their colors. The count and color drill was particularly good for these. The children enjoyed turning in pretty papers. Even more they liked seeing their work put on our bulletin board.

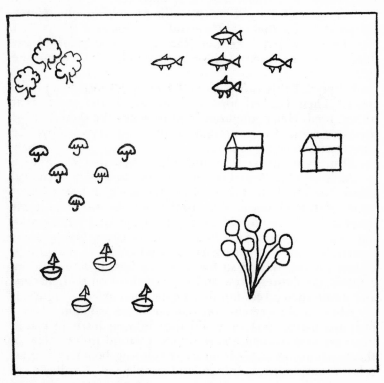

Copy, Count and Color   Figure 1

In asking questions during our actual periods of study, I saw many interesting reactions. Sometimes a child would respond as Felipe had. Again the same child might give a correct answer one day and an incorrect one the next. In some cases the child would simply bury his head at his desk and refuse to answer. The first time this happened I was stunned. Not knowing what to do, I asked the same question of another student. He answered correctly and to my utter amazement the first child peeped up at me and smiled as though he had answered my question.

At times I found my little ostriches could be coaxed into an answer; at other times they could simply be coaxed into looking up; sometimes they could not be budged. They would remain hidden until the lesson was completely over. This was particularly true of the mongoloids. Although they did not ordinarily respond in this manner, once they had "ducked," they usually stayed down.

Most children are eager to please their teacher. My group was no exception, so I was faced with another problem. Some of the children who continually raised their hands to answer questions seldom gave the correct answer. This worried me, not so much because the child did not know the answer, but rather because he was anticipating praise for his answer. When he was not praised, the look of disappointment was unmistakable in his eyes. Above all else I did not want my children to feel unimportant. If we were to progress together, each member of my class had to have recognition. As I learned the level of work in which each child performed best, my problem diminished. I formed individual questions designed for a specific child. When the child missed a question, he was soon given another, and still another, if necessary, until he gave the correct answer. Then he was happy and highly praised. We were both happy, too.

With my change from secondary to special education came still another problem. This had to do with the size and appearance of my students. To me, from my first day at school, they were normal, healthy-looking children. They

11

were happy children, some plump, some skinny, all friendly and affectionate. Some beautiful, with curly hair that put my permanent to shame; Sarah had lovely, tapering fingers; Sherry had wonderful, shadowy eyes and a cute, little, teen-age figure. Looking at the children it was difficult to realize they were mentally retarded.

In some cases I had still more trouble associating appearance with age. Nicky was twelve and very small for his age. Benny was the same age and over a foot taller. On the playground they were rough-and-tumble Indians. In class they were ever so far apart. Nicky's greatest delight was squeezing my hand. Benny was much happier teasing Sherry.

I found myself confused by size and age. As I look back on this, I see how easily one could be confused. I see also how unimportant these factors were. My only real problem was one of approach, what would be the best general attitude for my work in this field?

I had two ways in which to solve this problem. I could remember the ages, the IQs, and all the other stacks of information I had been given about each child. Perhaps this was the answer. I would know the child as a series of statistics, numbers, and reactions on certain tests. Somehow this did not appeal to me. During the first few weeks I used the general IQ level of the class as a basis for our level of work. Then I tossed that away along with the other statistics.

There was another choice and, unscientific though it was, I fell in line with it before I realized what had happened. My children and I were to be a family from eight-thirty until two o'clock every day. They were my flock and my responsibility, and we would grow together. There was one thing to remember always: they were still little children, pre-primer, regardless of age. We had to walk slowly. To the end of the school year I was still reminding myself of this.

Somehow we did walk slowly. We kept moving, and

always together. The children came to be my own, my pride, and my delight. Love, recognition, and individual importance replaced age, size, and statistics — facts that stayed hidden away in the back of my desk. I returned these records to the principal in June. To me they were well-kept charts and, as Shakespeare said of life, ". . . signifying nothing."

III THE GROWTH OF LEARNING is an intriguing process which teachers especially are privileged to observe. Perhaps this process is even more interesting in the field of the mentally retarded. We all have what we call our good and bad days. Things go smoothly one day and seem to fall apart the next. Children, too, have such days. One time it is easy to recall the right answer, it comes effortlessly. Another time the child's memory is hazy, and a simple answer escapes him. So it is with the average child.

With mentally retarded children the process of learning is the same, basic process; but it varies in so many respects that it is at times scarcely discernable as the same process. Repetition, for example, is an essential part of learning for any child. For the mentally retarded child it is more than an essential part of a process. It is the core of learning. Since the natural power of reasoning exists to a very limited degree for these children, they must learn by going over the same thing, again and again, until it becomes a part of their knowledge. One child will remember the days of the week; another will learn to count to twenty; a third child may do both. Thus there is a tremendous difference in the knowledge of these children although they may have the same intelligence level.

The normal learning process goes forward at varying degrees according to the individual. With mentally retarded children it is erratic. The learning process develops sporadically, sometimes going forward and sometimes retrogressing. With patience and kindness, and an enormous amount of repetition, the retarded child can learn. I know. I was privileged to watch their growth of learning. No great painting, no classical composition was ever so exciting, so rewarding.

I found that the process by which these children learn was not only erratic but also delicate and involved, like the complex workings of a tiny watch. A particle of dust in the right place will throw the watch out of balance. So, with my children, the slightest distraction affected their response in class. Needless to say there are many distractions in a classroom.

Noise, deliberate or inadvertent, played a large part in the response of a child. One day Ann volunteered to read some words from the board. As she was about to begin, Valentine coughed. Ann looked at him soberly.

"You got a cold? Cough drops in my desk," and she took out her cough drops to give to Valentine.

"No, something catch right here." The boy pointed to his throat.

"Go on. Take one." Valentine shook his head. Ann was upset by his reaction. She liked her cough drops and she wanted to help her classmate. She did not grasp the difference between a tickling in the throat and a sore throat. I sent Valentine downstairs for a drink of water, thanked Ann for being thoughtful, and returned to the words on the board. By this time, however, Ann had lost interest in reading. I could not really blame her, and certainly I could not correct her for having offered her cough drops. She was consistently and sincerely thoughtful, a quality I would hesitate to compare with reading words from a blackboard.

Another factor which often affected the response of a child was the attitude of his classmates. Countless times I have seen a child begin to read or count. Then he would suddenly stop to look around at his classmates. If they were watching attentively, the child would continue. If they did not seem to be interested, the child too would lose interest. Then the child, regardless of his familiarity with the work, would seem to become confused. He would answer incorrectly as his attention transferred from his recitation to his classmates.

Naturally my attitude and approach had a great deal to do with the manner in which the child responded.

"Marcille is going to read for us. Let's all pay close attention because Marcille reads so well." The little girl read very well, and I was anxious for the other children to become familiar with their new work. Marcille did not let me down. She read clearly and made only one mistake. After she had finished, several of the children volunteered to read the same page.

The next day before having the other children try the reading, I decided it would be a good review to have Marcille read it correctly again.

"Marcille, will you please read." She began to read but this time she missed several of the words, and halfway through the page she said she did not want to read anymore. This disturbed me. Later that day when the children were busy, I called Marcille up to the desk and we had a nice little chat. I praised her reading and told her how smart she was. Then I asked her why she had not wanted to finish her reading that day. She told me that the other children did not think she could do her work because I had asked her to read the same page again.

The third day I decided to try again, this time with a different approach.

"Marcille, I wonder if you would help me, please. I have to go over some papers; so while I'm busy, would you please start our reading? Let's pay close attention and see

16

how many of us can read this page as well as Marcille." She read the page without an error. Hands popped up all over the room. Everyone wanted to read as well as Marcille had read. After this episode I studied the children's responses and varied my approach according to each child.

Familiarity was another important factor in arousing a child's interest. Without a sense of familiarity the children were inattentive and easily distracted. Every child likes to feel that he is capable of performing the task before him. Most children are also a little venturesome and enjoy trying new things. Retarded children seem to be less prone in this direction. Thus I had to find ways of introducing new material without making the children feel overwhelmed. Repetition and familiarity with new material, this was quite a challenge.

Flash cards are a device probably familiar to everyone who ever went to school. When I was learning to read, I felt "the silly old cards the teacher held up" were dull. I much preferred to look at picture books — a little brown and white horse with a word beneath the picture, PONY. Unfortunately I am still depressed by flash cards. Naturally my class came to me well equipped, a set of flash cards for each reader, and there were five readers for the class. I was morose. I could not burn the cards; they were public property. It was certain that I would be excommunicated, jailed, or forced to suffer public humiliation. To add to my dilemma the flash cards had been called to my attention by a power higher than mine; they had been hailed as invaluable. I decided that "Discretion is the better part of — " something or other. Courageously I hauled out the flash cards and began to use them in class. The children were familiar with the cards, and I must admit that it was easy enough to slip in new words. We used the flash cards off and on all year. Later, however, to relieve their bleached appearance, the children cut out or drew pictures of words and we made a series of our own cards. (See chapter IV, Reading)

17

To vary the routine of the flash cards I used to copy the words on the board, putting in a new one here and there. The children enjoyed taking my pointer and going to the board to read. Other times I had them circle certain words and print their own names by the word. Eventually they learned to read the names of their classmates as well as their reading words.

Between the flash cards and the board work the children were progressing nicely. They said they liked to work at the board. It was "fun" and it was "not hard." So I added another new game, writing from the board. Many of the children had finished their printing books and still could not actually print. We began to list key words from our reader and from stories on the board. The children printed the words on their papers. Then they read the words aloud. This was a wonderful exercise, and by the end of the year they had progressed from copying words and phrases, to sentences and entire letters.

Another game which the children considered fun was a drawing game. I put two or three new words on the board, read the words with the children, and then asked them to draw a picture of one of the words, printing the word beneath the picture. The children were delighted. They loved to draw and color and enjoyed making new pictures. As fate would have it, I had never before personally progressed beyond the matchstick stage; but by the middle of the year I could produce a reasonable horse, cow, or pony. The draw, color, and print drill helped us all.

One of our favorite learning games was bingo. This was a new exercise with which the children were not familiar but one which they liked immediately. It was played with words instead of numbers. The words were new and old mixed together, and thus did not upset the children. Bingo was such fun that many times when the weather was bad and we were indoors for our play period, the children would ask to play bingo. Each time we played, I put the names of the winners on the board. At the end of the week the child who had won the most games received a candy bar. The candy bar was considered an enormous sign of success — success being edible, and short-lived.

Noise in the room, a lack of interest on the part of classmates, my attitude and approach, the unfamiliar — these are only a few of the factors which influenced the growth of learning in my group. Weather was another factor that played a consistently important part in the learning process.

I noticed that some days the children seemed to be particularly nervous, not one or two of them, but the entire class. After an especially hectic morning, I asked one of the teachers if her class had been difficult to handle that morning.

"Not difficult, just nervous," Mrs. Allen replied.

"How strange that you should have the same problem."

"Not at all, Margaret. It's the change in the weather."

"But why? Does that affect the children?" I asked.

"Always. Watch and you'll see. It's very interesting."

Mrs. Allen was right. The children changed with the weather. They seemed to be a part of nature, catching the wind and the rain and the thunderclouds somewhere inside, being blown and tossed, swept up or depressed by nature. I watched all year. The mood of the children and the weather were somehow related, to a remarkable extent I thought. There were pretty days of winter sunshine and gentle breezes when the children were restless, stirring, uneasy. Later in the day the weather turned cold, grey clouds darkened the sky, the change. The children knew and mysteriously felt the cold before it came. My other world, the one these children let me share, I so loved every part of it. When the weather changed, I was alone. Nature and the children were together sharing a strange and wonderful bond I could not understand.

Days, even weeks, sometimes passed by and our classroom activities continued with the usual degree of enthusiasm. Then a day came when, for some inexplicable reason, the

19

children were listless. They sat at their desks and looked sadly around the room. There was not anything they wanted to do. Their favorite games had no appeal. They seemed drained of energy and tired, like artificial flowers that need dusting. The first time this happened I tried to cheer them up. We had to have our studies, I told myself, so I must do something to stimulate the class.

I do not remember everything I tried, but I do recall struggling through our number work. After the ordeal was over, I was so much more listless than the children were that I decided life was too short to be lived that way. The learning process would have to wait. We abandoned our studies completely. After this first experience our depressed days were devoted entirely to the things we most enjoyed.

There were only a few days out of the year in which we did not study; but looking back on my experience at the Opportunity School, I think I cherish these few days more than any others. It was on these days, our little impromptu vacations, that we grew to know each other better. I put records on our phonograph, usually quiet, classical music which the children loved, and we sat and listened to the beautiful sounds. If the children felt like it, they colored in their coloring books. Some drew and colored their own pictures. A few looked at picture books. Later they listened to their favorite story records: "The Wooden Horse," "Frederick and the Dancing Leaf," "The Swan." They usually wanted to hear stories from a book, so I read to them. After the stories they discussed the characters. The children may have missed something by not being led through number work, reading, and writing; but I feel that what they missed in formal learning was more than compensated for by what they gained. Out of their discussion about different characters in the stories grew an awareness of right and wrong, how much better it was to be honest and truthful than to steal and tell stories, the virtue of kindness, the importance of understanding people.

As our discussions progressed, sad faces grew happy and

the children began to raise their hands to tell what they thought about different subjects. Each child contributed something, a word, a story, an idea, a part of his world. We grew closer together, and with that proximity came a greater understanding of one another. Our sad listless day became a happy one. The growth of learning was temporarily laid aside as we delighted in our brightly colored pictures, listened to beautiful music, examined human nature, and grew in understanding.

IV AS MY GROUP was educable, I had very specific plans for each day which always included the fundamental subjects: reading, writing, and numbers. In addition to these basic subjects, I taught the children science twice a week; and by late fall when the weather was definitely growing crisp, I had them ready for geography. Two times a week one of the other teachers, a trained speech therapist, came to my room for speech while I went to her class for music. It was my theory then, as it is today, that knowledge in any form, and especially for the retarded, is never wasted regardless of the effort demanded of the teacher, and in many cases the seemingly small progress and retention by the students. Besides the reading, writing, numbers, science, and speech, we had music, crafts, art, courtesy or manners, and safety.

Being a novice in special education I began the reading in September with a review of the alphabet and vowel sounds. To my delight some of the children knew the entire alphabet. By May some of them were still trying to learn it. Needless to say we did not spend nine months on the alphabet because some could learn and some could not. I reviewed them all a few minutes each day for several days, then we began to write a book.

Each child wrote his own. We discussed the circus which was coming to town in October and decided we wanted to write a book on animals. And so we began, A as in anteater, B as in bear, and so on. The children cut pictures from magazines, or drew their own if they did not find a picture they liked. We went through the entire alphabet. Each child wrote his book, made a cover for it of colored construction paper, as were the pages, and titled his book, "The Circus, by Ann" for example. When this feat was accomplished, I put the books on display in our room.

But the children and I were so proud of these books that displaying them before they were taken home did not seem adequate. Never having been a shy person, I brazenly, and apparently for the first time in the history of the school, summoned our principal. I must add in complete fairness that Miss Smith was principal of the adjoining elementary school, also. Naturally much of her time was taken up there. But Miss Smith came.

"I just want you to see what beautiful books these students have written." Miss Smith looked at me in stunned silence. Then the children all chimed in at once.

"Here's mine, Miss Smith. Read mine first."

Miss Smith finally smiled. She leafed through several books, praised each one, and promised to come back after school was out to read them all. The children were ecstatic. The next day we took our books to Mrs. Allen's room and let her group see them. They were most impressed as they were trainable in manual skills only, but they did enjoy the pretty pictures and bright pages.

To this day I am proud of the books. They were a project which took thirty to forty minutes work a day for several weeks, and from them came little bits and pieces of information that enriched our lives and increased our knowledge. Many of the animals the children knew very little about, so I brought encyclopedias. Using the simplest words possible, I read to the class, about Sarah's anteater, for instance. Then Sarah took her picture around again to each student.

23

We had made a new friend at the zoo, which I had planned as a field trip in the spring. The children knew that they might not see the anteater at the circus, but they would meet him in the spring at the zoo.

Several weeks remained before the circus, so we began another project in preparation for our trip to the circus.

Here I should add that the tickets to the circus were donated to the Opportunity School so that each child, regardless of his financial status, could attend. We had in our room a rectangular table with four-inch high edges that surrounded the surface. We decided to build a circus! And this we did. There were cages made of construction paper or strips of carton pasted together. These were painted with tempra paints. The bars for the cages were of pipe cleaners or more strips of construction paper. Each child decided how he wanted his cage to be made. Each student picked a partner — this was always great fun, to get to choose, or to be chosen — and our circus was under way. I brought sand for the sawdust, and in several weeks we had our circus ready. Some children molded animals from clay. Others cut out pictures and made stands for them. The names of the animals were put on the board so that each cage or wagon had a neatly printed sign identifying its occupant. The last, and most difficult part for me, was manufacturing a Big Top. My wonderful boys had many ideas but none was too practical. In the end we braced wooden poles inside the table and tied a large red cloth to the poles. Our circus had a top. Now all that remained was the audience.

Miss Smith was, of course, invited at once to come see. This she did and heartily approved. I made certain the children had their writing tablets open to our circus words and simple sentences. In addition one of the readers had a circus story. The flash cards for the story were on prominent display, plus some cards that the children had made. There was a one-page story about a giraffe that I had written on the board. Each child had copied it neatly. These stories

24

were on the bulletin board. This was obviously not busy work. The children were surrounded by learning activities and loving every minute of it.

Besides Miss Smith, each room in the Opportunity School was invited to visit, and each one came. Our circus was so nice that we left it up several weeks during which time our Open House was scheduled. The parents were stunned. Their children were quoting little things about the animals: where they lived, how they ate, whether they were dangerous or friendly and so forth. Their giraffe stories were very neatly printed, and there was a huge vocabulary list of flash cards. Not every child could read every word, of course, nor could each child print perfectly straight letters; but each one was a part of our project, each had something to be proud of. And I was the most proud of all. My little family, handicaps and all, had made a circus. Now all that remained was to attend the actual performance.

While all this was going on the children were still working in their own readers, by group, according to their level. I had four basic groups and each child read to me individually every day. Thus it was a simple matter to check their mastery of the Red Book, for instance, then move a child, as he progressed, to the next level. Tests, as such, were not used. I reviewed flash cards, discussed the stories, and then when I felt the child had gained as much as he could from his particular reader, I moved him on. This was always done with praise. He was welcomed into the new group with great delight by his friends. Stars were put on a reading chart. Rewards — always rewards — never disapproval. Stars for the flash cards, stars for the stories, stars for spelling the basic words. Not one child was without many, many stars. This was not a world of fierce competition, such as the business world, but there was competition of a kind. It was a gentle sort of thing, an intangible feeling of pride. And as my family and I grew together, some in knowledge, all in trust, the children tried harder to succeed.

25

These stars were precious goals. Not each truly signified the mastery of a certain piece of work; but what it lacked in mastery, as we think of this word in our world, it more than made up for in effort, in their world of limitations and handicaps.

WRITING

This subject would better be described as printing because retarded children have many problems, not a few of which are often motor connected. I soon discovered that it was much more difficult for the children to use their printing books than it was for them to copy work that I put on the board. Those who could use the books were encouraged to do so. I found that the more they copied, be it a tree or a flash-card word, the better and stronger their letters became. Any activity which required their using hand tools — pencil, crayola, scissors, paint brush, ruler — helped them. My personal goal for the group was that each be able to print his name, address, city, state, and phone number. I felt that this was certainly directly related to their safety. Also I knew that a few from my group would eventually get jobs. They were trainable in the line of simple, rote-type labor. They would need to be able to fill out basic information. If the first or second grade dropout, or the non-English-speaking individual could get employment, some of my children who could read from elementary readers and print rudimentary information could surely get jobs too. Of course the pay would be low and the work simple; but they would be partially independent, and they would be contributing something to their family's income. Thus we spent much time practicing this one skill which, in the outside world we perform so often, and so seldom realize how fortunate we are. My goal for each one of the children was never completely fulfilled, but each did learn to write his first and last name. By early spring some five or six could write their complete address.

26

From this world in which I spent nine months, I learned the virtue of patience, the reward of a smile, the miracles that feeling loved can bring, and the tremendous importance of motivation. But motivation for a retarded child has to come in a tangible and immediate form, one that he can see and touch right now. It is not the motivation of high school where the student is earning a credit, or preparing for college, or even doing his work without a goal, simply doing it because his teacher says to do it or he will fail. These are motivating factors for the "average" child, not the retarded. I want to add here that after eleven years' teaching, ten of which were in public junior and senior high school, I am still waiting to meet my first average child. Simply put, there is no such person.

So I had the problem of what I call here-and-now motivation. I think my biggest single source of help came from an idea I had which, to one unfamiliar with the limitations of these students, sounds utterly absurd, more so, perhaps, to one familiar with them. I told the children that we were practicing our writing especially hard this fall because later in the year we were going to have **Pen Pals!** This idea was totally new to them. They did not understand it but with Teacher so happy and excited about it, they knew it was something good. I explained the entire idea simply and carefully. They were delighted. We did our writing carefully each day, sometimes just practicing the date and the salutation of a letter. From time to time we wrote each other. This was a huge success.

"Look, Teacher, Bobby wrote me a letter." The fact that the letter was copied from the board and each student put in his friend's name did not matter. Lack of originality never bothered the children. They were happy with recognition and any manifestation of affection.

In May of the school year we wrote our letters. They went to a school similar to ours in Los Angeles. The children in California answered almost by return mail. I cannot adequately describe the delight and pride my children felt. They read their letters aloud, some needed help. This did not matter. They took the letters around to each classmate, they put them on our display table (formerly a circus, then in rapid succession a Pilgrim Village, Santa's Toy Shop, a Valentine Factory, and an Easter scene), and at last they took the letters home. Those wonderful letters from their Pen Pals! (Figure 2)

NUMBERS

Certainly, if my children were to achieve some independence regardless of how small it might be, they had to have a basic familiarity with numbers. Math is involved in so many things we do each day that it would be virtually impossible to get along without it. Even simple directions involve numbers. "Turn to page three," but how can a child do this without knowing what the figure three is? "Bring me two spoons, please." The child might want to help set the table at home, but what does the word two represent? "What time is it?" How dreadful to go through life not being able to answer such simple questions, or follow such easy directions. Definitely my group had to have a lot of number work. Thus I had the problem of where to begin and how to make it fun.

I started with a simple, oral review of counting from one to ten. Nearly every child could do this. We practiced with different objects in the room. We even counted each other. We lined up by numbers just for fun on certain days. This was quite successful, as each student had to remember his number and put himself in line at the proper place, five comes after four and before six. From this activity we turned to board work. First we practiced copying the numbers in order; next we tried writing them from memory. More rewards, which meant more stars. Each day that a child could write even one number further, he added another star to his math chart. At one time during the fall all of

Dear friends,
　　We send you this
letter from Austin
Opportunity Shool.
We want to hear
about your school and

Disorder: Brain damage and cerebral palsy　　Figure 2

Dear Friends,
We send you this letter from Austin Opportunity School. We want to hear about your school and

Disorder: Brain damage, cause unknown   Figure 2

Dear Friends,
    We send you this
letter from Autin
Opportunity School. .
We wantto hear
about your school and

Disorder: Cephalic   Figure 2

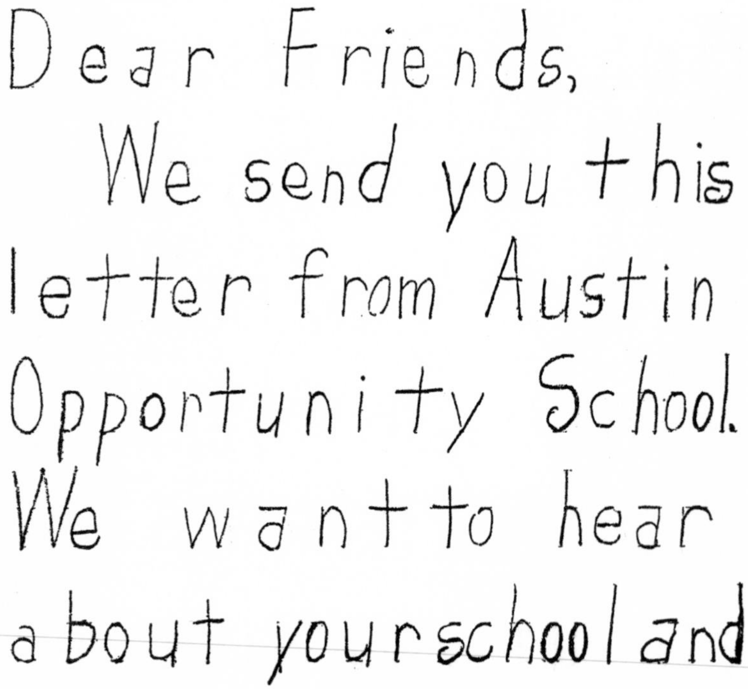

Dear Friends,
  We send you this letter from Austin Opportunity School. We want to hear about your school and

Disorder: Brain damage caused by excessive fever over a prolonged period of time

Figure 2

Dear Friends,
We send youthis
letter fromAustin
Opportunity School.
Wewant to hear
about yourschool and

Disorder: Mongolism   Figure 2

the children could write to ten. Later in the year some forgot, or would leave out a number; so that, although we went on to other number work, we continued our basic one-to-ten drill.

After this I introduced a small and large grouping activity. It was a variation of the copy, count, and color exercise which the children all enjoyed. "Copy three small boats and two large balloons. Make them any color you like." There might be five small boats and four large balloons on the board but the child only copied three of one kind and two of the other. Later they wrote the numbers under the pictures. Then they were asked to count all of the figures. Thus they learned that three and two equal five. After weeks of drill from one to ten I decided the children should start working toward twenty. They did this very well and most of the class learned to write to twenty. I did not attempt any large addition. The answer always had to be twenty or below.

One day, strictly for fun, I asked how many would like to write all the numbers to one hundred. Every hand went up. So, with a simple chart on the board, they began to write to a hundred. I knew this was a task that no more than one or two children could actually learn, but it was an excellent drill for dexterity, and it was good practice in using the ruler. (Figure 3)

From this drill I proceeded to a height chart. This involved the use of a yardstick, or the Big Ruler as some of them called it. The children chose partners and measured each other. I added their answers, such as thirty-six inches and sixteen inches, and I wrote the number by each student's name. It was great fun for the children. I think up until this activity in class, the children had always been checked by the school nurse for height and weight. Now, at least, they understood something about the process and they learned the meaning of a new word, measure, meaning how long or how high.

These little extra activities which we did for fun, I

1	2	3	4	5	6	7	8	9	10
11	12	13	1	1	1	1			2
21	22	3	4	5					3
3									40
4									50
5									0
6									0
7									0
8									0
9									10 ↓

Figure 3

explained them to the children as rewards, in no way interfered with the basic skills. The children had number books and they worked in these throughout the year. Besides these workbooks, we had flash cards and we made flash cards. They enjoyed making their own, sometimes with numbers and sometimes with pictures. I liked this activity, too. It gave them practice in cutting out pictures and pasting them on construction paper. It was a counting activity which helped their little fingers grow stronger, and it gave the children a feeling of recognition. I put their flash cards on two large rings, so that I could flip the pages quickly and easily. Every few days I would work the set in as a review. "Count the boats, count the airplanes," and so on. Never once did I not hear one or two whispers, "That's my picture Teacher has now." But the basic skill of addition was always present, either from the workbook, from flash cards, or from the board. Frequently I put number work on the board with the directions to copy and find the right answer. (Figure 4)

As we had worked in size relationships, large and small, big and little, now we began to expand our knowledge of grouping. We studied pairs, bunches, and pounds. The children brought magazines and cut out pictures. They counted the objects in each group. When the pictures were of simple objects, I put short word lists on the board, and they printed the name under the picture, three apples, four lemons, or two cakes. They learned that a pair is always two, a group could be any number. The children loved to play Teacher, so each would have his turn in front of the class with his pictures. He called on different members of the class. It was great fun; and while they were learning about pairs and groups and pounds, they were also practicing their speech, and, most important gaining a feeling of recognition.

At this point in our number work I introduced simple fractions. I did not do this with the thought of teaching fractions as one would do in an arithmetic class in ele-

$$\begin{array}{r} 1 \\ +\,1 \\ \hline 2 \end{array} \qquad \begin{array}{r} 1 \\ +\,2 \\ \hline 3 \end{array} \qquad \begin{array}{r} 2 \\ +\,3 \\ \hline 5 \end{array} \qquad \begin{array}{r} 3 \\ +\,2 \\ \hline 5 \end{array}$$

$$\begin{array}{r} 2 \\ +\,2 \\ \hline 4 \end{array} \qquad \begin{array}{r} 1 \\ +\,3 \\ \hline 4 \end{array} \qquad \begin{array}{r} 2 \\ +\,4 \\ \hline 6 \end{array} \qquad \begin{array}{r} 3 \\ +\,3 \\ \hline 6 \end{array}$$

$$\begin{array}{r} 3 \\ +\,3 \\ \hline 6 \end{array} \qquad \begin{array}{r} 1 \\ +\,4 \\ \hline 5 \end{array} \qquad \begin{array}{r} 2 \\ +\,5 \\ \hline 7 \end{array} \qquad \begin{array}{r} 3 \\ +\,4 \\ \hline 7 \end{array}$$

$$\begin{array}{r} 4 \\ +\,4 \\ \hline 8 \end{array} \qquad \begin{array}{r} 1 \\ +\,5 \\ \hline 6 \end{array} \qquad \begin{array}{r} 2 \\ +\,6 \\ \hline 8 \end{array} \qquad \begin{array}{r} 3 \\ +\,5 \\ \hline 8 \end{array}$$

$$\begin{array}{r} 5 \\ +\,5 \\ \hline 10 \end{array} \qquad \begin{array}{r} 1 \\ +\,6 \\ \hline 7 \end{array} \qquad \begin{array}{r} 2 \\ +\,7 \\ \hline 9 \end{array} \qquad \begin{array}{r} 3 \\ +\,6 \\ \hline 9 \end{array}$$

Figure 4

mentary school. Rather I thought that the basic idea of one-half and one-half making up one whole unit would be helpful. I knew some of the children could grasp the idea, were they exposed to it, and some could not. Thus we turned to Teacher's big, red apple. I demonstrated by cutting it in two, then holding the halves together again. After this we drew and colored halves, then the whole. Under the work the children copied one-half plus one-half — equals one. We came back to this idea during the remainder of the year. We used lemons, oranges, grapefruits and just about anything disectable and edible. The special reward for that particular day was naturally a piece of Teacher's lunch.

As Christmas approached, we had more and more discussion about what Santa might bring. I decided that this would be a good time to bring in dollars and cents and the symbols for each. We used play money and practiced the dollar or cent mark in our number work. I did not attempt decimals. Perhaps I should have; but I had in mind a grocery store project for early spring, and I felt that with the play money and toy cash register, the basic idea of the decimal would come more easily and in a more tangible sense. It did.

After Christmas and before the grocery store project, I began simple subtraction. It was great fun to copy, count, and color three apples from the board, for example, then be called upon to go to the board and circle the remaining apples. Thus the children eased into such simple fundamentals as five minus three equals two. Gradually we worked our way up to ten. Paralleling this board work were the drills in their workbooks, plus a large amount of one favorite activity, counting and subtracting each other: if you counted Sarah, Felipe, and Marcille, then subtracted Felipe (he was allowed to stand by me so that he surely would not feel left out), then you could easily see that three minus one equals two. This type activity was very good for the children. Not only was it a live demonstration of the number concept but also it was a means of releasing a little energy in class by moving about in an orderly fashion.

After basic subtraction, up to ten, I felt the children had earned their reward — the grocery store! We played this for days, and each day we enjoyed it more. This special child with whom I worked for nine months was special in many ways. Not only because tests and charts and reports showed him to be exceptional on paper, but also because his personality was exceptional, too. He was slow to anger, quick to be hurt, and always ready to respond to warmth and love. I add this because in our grand game of Grocery Store, we continued to play a few minutes each day until each child had been the grocer in charge of the cash register, each one had been the clerk who read the labels and located the purchases, and each one had filled a shopping list, paid for the items with play money, and counted his change.

This was the end result of our work the past fall. The effort was well worth it. Each had a part in the store, and each one played a role. The children loved bringing empty cans and boxes, all of which had to be marked in cents. They enjoyed grouping items: vegetables, staples, meat products. They liked wearing the white butcher's apron I borrowed from our own grocer, as they worked the cash register. They deserved a reward, especially one in which they could use their new skills. I hoped at the time that later in life some of my family would be given a chance to use at least part of their knowledge. Each was so willing; few were so able. This was our world of cotton candy and carrousels. What would that other, outside world be like? I so desperately wanted to prepare them.

The last major project I undertook for the children was telling time. In mid-November Nicky had a birthday! My shy, little boy who had helped me through my first day of school with his words, "I like you, Teacher," came scooting into class on this special day.

"Look, Teacher, my daddy sent me a watch." Almost before I thought, it popped out.

"Nicky, it's beautiful. Let's learn to tell time."

"Can we, Teacher, can we?"

"Of course, Nicky. We'll start today," and so we did. Nicky showed us all his watch, which was a beautiful gift his father had sent from overseas. That day the children drew circles in their tablets, with the tops from paste jars. Then, following my board work, they practiced writing from one to twelve around the circle. The next day we all drew big and little hands, beginning at one o'clock. Thereafter we progressed an hour a day until we reached noon, lunch time. This had meaning. Next we took up the half hours, and finally for the few who could learn it, the quarter hours. It was fun.

I made a clock out of a paper plate. The children took turns coming to the front of the room and setting my clock. We practiced this activity throughout the year. At last I brought an old alarm clock from home. What bedlam we had when the alarm went off! That was surely a reward day, and the one who guessed the time had a piece of candy at lunch. Needless to say guess-and-tell-the-time was one of the children's favorite games.

The one other number concept I introduced during the year was really more a fun idea and more geometrically related than mathematically. Not being in the slightest way talented artistically, I found myself using geometric forms to put our counting lessons on the board:

As the children progressed, I used the forms more and more, and began to use their correct names. Something that was round was called a circle, for example. Onto circles we drew tails and counted balloons. From triangles we made slices of pie and colored and counted these. Squares made the beginning of a Jack-in-the-box, and the rectangle was the same shape as a cage in our circus. Not all of the children learned these words; we did not try to spell them, but at least each child could point to the form when I said the word. It seemed important to me, as so many simple things are related to these shapes — a traffic light is round, to name only one. So, with these basic and varied concepts in their simplest forms, I based our year's work with numbers. The children enjoyed our work. Numbers were fun, and their delight was perhaps my biggest reward. Math had been my most difficult subject in college. To make it fun for my special family at the Opportunity School was pure delight.

WE LEARN FROM OTHER SUBJECTS

In the fall I began science. This subject was actually a combination of botany, biology, and general information.

We began by making notebooks on vegetables. We had two main classes, those that grow above and below the ground. From the board the children copied and colored turnips, carrots, potatoes and so on. I was careful to include the ground level with each picture. Next we drew vegetables that grow above the ground. We had lettuce, peas, cabbages — the children named the vegetable, I put it on the board, and it went in our vegetable book. As they copied and colored, we discussed the best climate for that particular vegetable, how it was planted — by seed, root, kernel — and finally how it was sold in the store — by the pound, by the bunch, by the stalk. When we finished our vegetable books, and they were taken home, we began the study of flowers. These special children seemed to me to have a closer relationship with nature, color, and sound than the average child. Perhaps because the boundaries of their world are much

41

more limited than are those of our world, sight and sound are of tremendous importance. The children enjoyed making these notebooks, so we continued our science lessons once or twice a week throughout the year. We proceeded from vegetables and flowers to trees, animals (which worked in very well with our circus), and fish.

One day as the children were copying a polar bear, Felipe said, "I know where he lives, Teacher. He lives where it's very cold and there's snow on the ground."

"That's right, Felipe. That's very interesting."

"How do you know that?" Anne asked.

"Because I saw a picture on T.V." The children were busily copying and coloring and talking about snow and polar bears.

"Tell me, Felipe," I asked, "where is it very cold all of the time?"

"I can't remember the name but on T.V. it said there was always snow, and it showed pictures."

It occurred to me during this conversation that the children could learn a little bit about geography and thus make the things they saw and heard more meaningful. In a large storeroom across the hall from me I found a framed, hard-back map, perhaps four feet wide and three feet high. It could easily be seen by each child if it were used in a grouped semicircle. What a fun experience for the children, I thought, to sit around a big map and see where they lived and where the climate was cold or hot, to talk about our weather, about fishing, and vegetables, and flowers. I felt the map had unlimited possibilities. I could see how our understanding might grow. Since the map was old and dusty it was surely not being used in the Opportunity School. I simply borrowed it — permanently, I thought at the time. Thus our geography class began. I had colored thumb tacks, one for each state. I had large printed names with the same color thumb tacks around the border of the map. We began by sitting in a semicircle. Each child got to select a name with its colored tack and try to locate it on the map. We all clapped when the student found his state. He then got to put the name in place, tell the color of the tack, and repeat the name of the state after me. This was a good drill on colors and it gave each child oral practice before the group. I added snow to the map and invited the teacher next to me to come tell us about living "where it's cold." Mrs. Miller was a charming young teacher from New York who had taught special education previously. She knew exactly what the children would enjoy — mittens, snowball fights, sleds, furry animals. We all thoroughly enjoyed her visit.

As I had lived in Mexico, it was easy to bring sombreros, jewelry, leather goods, and a Mexican blouse and skirt. We had located Mrs. Miller and the snow in the North. Now we located Teacher and Mexico in the South. The children were grasping the idea of direction. They were using new words to tell stories; some of them began to watch the weather map on T.V. and talk about rain and floods. One of the boys received a rod and reel for his birthday, so we discussed water and fishing. We had geography twice a week and the children thoroughly enjoyed it. Even my two little mongoloid girls who were rather shy about talking before the class began to point and ask questions. The class was going very well. Then one morning in late November as we were grouped around our map discussing Santa Claus, and the snow, and his reindeer, my principal came into our room. It was to be her shortest visit all year. She took one glance at the map and called me into the hall.

"Get that map out of your room. Don't you know these children are retarded? They can't be taught regular subjects. The next time you decide to teach something different be sure you check with me first."

She was gone for the day and my little geography class was over for the year. It had lasted exactly one month. To this day I am still not convinced that my principal's decision was the right one. I knew these children could learn geography to a limited degree. I knew it could be

43

meaningful. I knew this was a fact because I saw my class do it!

Every Friday I read the children a Bible story. There were several reasons for this. To begin with by Friday afternoon the children were tired. They enjoyed just sitting quietly and hearing a story. The Bible is full of colorful stories about animals and children. Usually there is a moral to the story. After reading it to them the children would draw and color a picture from the story while I played quiet music on the phonograph, usually something classical.

It was a nice way to begin the weekend. The following Monday we always played a little game of recall. "Who can tell me what our story was about last Friday?" Each child had a chance to say something, maybe he only wanted to say a few words, sometimes several sentences. He was practicing recall without knowing it. After this we discussed different Sunday School lessons. Nearly every child attended Sunday School, and with surprising regularity, so I used this as another means of recall. The weekend was an eventful time, so if a child had not answered several times during our discussion, then I asked him about what he did Saturday or Sunday. He was still practicing recall as well as speech. The mind had to be stretched and stimulated. Our Monday morning discussion was only one of many ways to do this.

By the middle of the year I was so deeply involved in my new world that simply teaching these children at school was no longer my only concern. I knew their families by now, fathers and mothers, brothers and sisters. I asked for permission to send home a progress report to each family on report card day. Fortunately this idea was acceptable. For the remainder of the year my students had their own cards on that special day. The students loved taking things home. The first time I did this the reaction was surprising. Several parents came into my room to thank me. They had been to my room nearly every day for four months. They were always welcome. We discussed their children almost

44

daily — and sometimes personal, family problems. But the report card was a new idea. Now the family could discuss grades and progress together. No one was left out. I sent home these reports for the rest of the year. (Figure 5)

```
                              School......................
                              Section.....................
                              Date........................

Report of...........................
             This report is sent to each parent to give a
general idea of your child's progress. Please remember
that  no child is expected to progress in all fields
each reporting period.

                    .........................

Behavior............
Manners.............
Courtesy............
Socialization.......
Attention...........
Reading.............
Writing.............
Numbers.............
Speech..............
Art.................
Music...............
General progress....
```

Figure 5

V RETARDED CHILDREN have a gentle, aesthetic side to their nature. They live in a shadowy world in which color and sound play an important part, spark their imagination. As it is a limited world nonetheless of here-and-now, of see-and-touch, it is also a world of what you and I might call pretend. It is a world of fantasy in which stories of dragons are real and emotion in any form is constant, always sparked by the same story. For instance no matter how often my children heard "Little Red Riding-hood," there were still cries of "He's going to eat her" when we got poor Red Ridinghood as far as her grandmother's house. At the end of the story after the woodsman saved the girl, all of the children clapped loudly. The story had a happy ending and the children were glad. They had just been through an emotional experience, and they felt relief and joy that everything was all right again. They needed to clap to release their tension. Ordinary children in Kinder-garten might be momentarily caught up in the plight of Red Ridinghood, but afterward they would surely question the plausibility of such a story and its ever actually taking place. Not so with my group. The children discussed how bad the wolf was and how nice Red Ridinghood was to take her sick grandmother a basket of goodies; the wolf and the girl were very much alive to these children. They enjoyed drawing pictures after the story-record. The wolf might appear in several of the children's pictures; sometimes he was red, sometimes brown. More interesting still was Red Ridinghood. Her dress was almost any color imaginable, but her hood was always red. That was her name. It was a color all sixteen of the children knew; it was repeated throughout the story. It was vivid, it was here and now, it was a living experience, it was repetition; the children loved it. With the familiar, they were secure. They never tired of their story-records, nor of drawing pictures of them.

We all have our old favorites — dresses, foods, records. So, too, did my class. Among their story-music records they liked "Peter and the Wolf," "Swan Lake," "Sleeping Beauty," and "Treasure Island" better than the others. They enjoyed all of them, but these four were their favorites. I include these specific selections because the illustrations which follow were some of the best work the children did all year. They were drawn in January, so that the children were quite familiar with the stories by this time. Each drawing was made several days apart. All of the pictures follow the same order: 1) "Peter and the Wolf," 2) "Swan Lake," 3) "Sleeping Beauty," 4) "Treasure Island." (Figure 6)

In addition to the story-record which was strictly a story on record such as "Little Red Ridinghood" or "Bugs Bunny in Fairyland," and the story-music record, "Peter and the Wolf," and the aforementioned records, there was a third type record which was music only. No story was told. The children surprised me with their reactions to this latter type. They enjoyed it thoroughly and frequently requested it during our art or music period. Sometimes they would illustrate the music; other times they colored in their coloring books while the record was playing. One day I asked all of the children to draw a picture for "The Blue Danube," one of their favorites. I saved these drawings; and later in the week I returned them to the children, praised them highly, and asked the children to draw a picture for

47

Peter and the Wolf   Figure 6

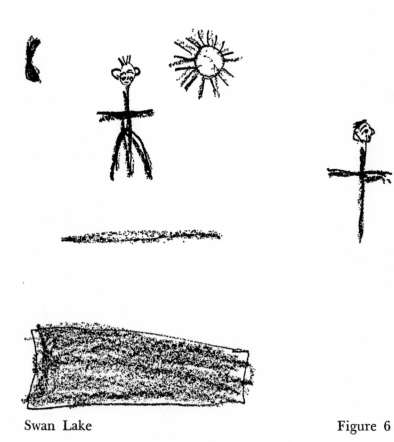

Swan Lake   Figure 6

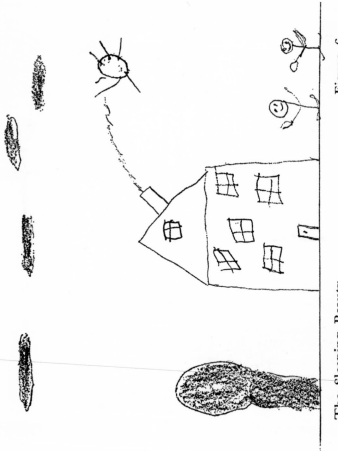

The Sleeping Beauty

Figure 6

Treasure Island   Figure 6

"The Parade of the Wooden Soldier," was another of their favorites. These drawings came strictly from the children's imagination and the music as there was no story with the record, and I did not tell them one. I explained only that the Blue Danube was a river far away in another country. (Figure 7) I think these pictures are interesting to compare with the story-music illustrations. The former are far more concrete, being here and now, sound and story, listen and experience.

The Blue Danube   Figure 7

The children had many other favorite records either for listening or in conjunction with our art. The two Biblical records they enjoyed most were the story of "Daniel in the Lion's Den" and "David and Goliath." These I usually saved for Friday or Monday. They worked in very nicely with our recall discussions. Our other principal music projects were learning and singing songs, and our rhythm band. Sometimes I used records with our band, other times singing. By Christmas the children had learned several nice songs, so with the bells, drum, triangle and symbol, we went caroling to the other five rooms. We all enjoyed this. It was a joyous sharing in the true spirit of Christmas.

In addition to drawing pictures of stories, or coloring in their color books, I had many other art-connected drills

52

The Parade of the Wooden Soldiers   Figure 7

for the children without music. With rulers and paste tops, for example, we practiced triangles, rectangles, squares, and circles. This was really a number-work exercise but many times, after the children learned their primary colors, I used it to have them practice other colors: pink, orange, purple, light blue, dark green, and so on. By the end of the year most of my group knew eight or ten colors. It seemed important to me for the children to know that grapes are light green or purple. It surely would be useful if a child were sent to the store with a shopping list. With the circle I had the children draw bunches of grapes and color them. The color and word was printed beneath the picture. So, from a simple geometric drill in art we progressed through colors, to pictures, printing, and reading.

Besides this copy exercise I often had the children trace pictures. This drill is far more difficult than the ordinary person realizes. Many of my children had motor or visual problems or both. In tracing a simple object or an animal both hands are involved as well as vision. This was a new exercise for the children and at first they did not do well. Later in the year some of them became quite good at it. To encourage the children I had them color their pictures and mount them on colored construction paper. Thus the tracing exercise led to using paste neatly on the back edge of the picture and mounting their work in the center of the colored paper. The picture had a border. The children liked these colored borders; their work looked pretty, and they were proud of it. So the tracing drill became familiar to my group, and each time they did it they tried a little harder to make it pretty. One little girl in my group had cerebral palsy to a minor degree. This exercise was terribly difficult for her. I worked with her closely all year, always making certain that the picture she traced was large and simple. I saved her work in my desk. One day in the spring after a tracing drill I quietly called her up to my desk. There were her pictures from the previous fall spread out for her to see.

54

"Look, Sherry. Which picture is the best?" She pointed to the one she had just done which really was quite good.

"Now look at these others. Did you know how lovely your work is now? I want you to take all of these pictures home and show your mommy and daddy how much you have improved." I stapled the pictures together in order and Sherry took them home. The next afternoon her mother and stepfather came to my room after school. They were both visibly and emotionally upset, or so they appeared to me.

The mother told me that they had brought Sherry to the Opportunity School as a last resort. They had taken her to specialists and therapists; they had her in private schools; anything they thought of or had recommended to them they had tried. They had gotten no encouragement that Sherry would ever improve, be able to print her name legibly, or take part in any average activities.

"I knew Sherry liked school," her mother said, "and we felt like she was making progress from the work she's brought home; but until yesterday when she showed us her tracing pictures, we were afraid to hope."

There was a long pause in the conversation. I was stunned by what I had heard, and the little girl's parents were so deeply involved that they could hardly talk about her. She was a truly beautiful child, a sweet, quiet girl about twelve years old. To look at she was normal in every way. She was even beginning to develop a figure. How tragic to have this lovely child and be totally discouraged wherever you turned for help. I wondered to myself what all of these specialists had tried, but this was not for one to ask. Sherry responded willingly in class, her reading was in the upper group, her speech and writing were improving. In fact, she was one of my more advanced students. Surely she was educable. She was beautifully mannered, kind, and considerate. She was a child to be loved and enjoyed as any other child. These things I could and did tell Sherry's parents.

Our year's work in art was not all drawing, tracing, and

coloring. The children enjoyed working with clay. Each one brought a twenty-five-cent box of clay from the dime store and we rolled it, flattened it, drew on it with pencils, cut out forms from it with scissors, made figures of each other and, in short, we did everything but eat it.

All of this was particularly good for the children with weak fingers. One day after listening to "Hansel and Gretel," Benny asked if we could use clay. From this suggestion grew one of our display projects. The children liked the record so much that I asked them if they would like to make the story in clay. Benny, Wayne, Frances — every hand went up. Thus we began a new project. The children worked on the house, the witch, the boy and girl and the forest for several weeks. When they were finished, all of the figures were put in place on our display table, and of course we invited our neighbors to come visit. Each room came on a different day. The children were invited to hear the record, then see the story. I had several different helpers each day, so that by the end of the week each child had been an important part of our project, making and displaying. He had contributed and related. He was a necessary part of our class. Here I add that I would almost defy anybody to find an individual, totally competent or limited, who does not need to feel necessary. I surely do and so did my children.

In addition to coloring and clay we had sewing and crafts. The sewing was kept very simple. It was usually done on large cardboard pictures, with holes punched around the edges, such as are sold in the dime store. The children had large needles with a rounded, safe end and a large eye. The pictures were outlined with different shades of brightly colored yarn.

For a change from this activity I brought a box of buttons of all shapes, sizes, and colors from home. I had the children string and knot these and make bracelets or necklaces for their mothers and sisters. Later in the year I took up simple braiding with rug yarn. From this activity I let

56

the children make hair bands and with colored cord, jewelry, such as large pinwheels which were glued together in a circle, then glued on a flat bar with the pin attached to the other side. These, too, made attractive little gifts for the children to take home. These sewing and braiding crafts were wonderful drills for finger and visual control. A few of the children still could not tie shoelaces. The more I had them do manual-visual exercises, the better it was for their own printing, tying, and buttoning.

Craftwork was another part of our art that the children enjoyed, especially since their work was always on our bulletin board or displayed on our big table; I never decorated the bulletin board even one time throughout the year. It was their board and the children did the work. I want to add that it was a very colorful board and so filled with their work that I finally had to move their charts with their stars to another place in our room.

Any holiday was a wonderful reason to have crafts. At Thanksgiving I had the children make stand-up turkeys and pilgrims from a simple pattern I found in a magazine. I put these all around the room, on the chalk trays, window sills and display table. They were made of construction paper and colored appropriately. The day vacation began I sent them home, and many of the parents told me they used them on their table for Thanksgiving dinner. I knew how pleased the children were. Their pumpkins and witches for Halloween had been cute, little pin-up decorations, but the Pilgrims and turkeys were much better.

As the Christmas season approached, more and more of our work was related to Santa: printing, counting, reading flash cards, and certainly our crafts. I found easy-to-make cutouts of Santa. This time, however, the children made beards of cotton and pasted them to the faces. Next they cut out Christmas pictures from magazines and mounted them on red or green doubled construction paper. Inside they printed neatly "Merry Christmas and Happy New Year" and signed their names. Several of the children had time to make more than one card. After the Santas and the cards were finished and on display, we started our Christmas presents. I began by giving the boys and girls a choice of which they wanted to make, cookie cans or dish towels with painted flowers. The children were so excited and worked so well that by the time the holidays came each child had made both gifts. The cookie cans were made from coffee cans with plastic lids. I brought paints and decals and the children selected their favorite color and decal. These turned out very nicely and I carefully hid them in our cloakroom to be wrapped the last day before vacation. The dish towels were a little more involved. The children brought clean towels of a flat material from home. They had to trace their designs on the towels, then paint them on and let them dry. Later I pressed them which was to set the paint. The towels, too, came out quite well, and I hid these with the cookie cans. It was a very happy season with much controlled activity. Our subjects were still going on, but at this particular season craftwork was our favorite.

At Easter I helped the children make bunnies with fluffy tails, weave baskets of colored paper for table decorations, make Easter cards, and decorate crosses. All of their projects were sent home the day vacation began. Easter and our crafts were not so involved as was Christmas, but we did spend more time on it than on Valentine's Day. For the latter I used heart patterns of different sizes and showed the children how to make double, connecting Valentines. After this was done, I put several four-line verses on the board, read them aloud, and had everyone select his favorite. The children printed the verse neatly on tablet paper, cut it out, and pasted it inside the heart.

Again the more rapid workers had time to make several valentines, but every child made at least one and it was displayed and praised.

In closing this chapter on art and music I must add one sadly humorous fact. The nearest I personally ever came to failing a subject was a compulsory seventh grade art course.

At the end of the year my teacher took a leave of absence, and left the country for six months, probably to recover from me. I have always felt that she simply was not taking any chance that she have me for a pupil the next year. She need not have worried. That was my last art course ever. The next year I took Latin, another form of torture, but at least it was not the same type. I did not have to display my gross ineptitude to my classmates. How ironic that twelve years later I was to spend an entire year teaching and using art every day — and enjoying every minute of it.

V I ONE OF THE FIRST things I began to work into our lessons was safety. We talked about it in class, we made stop signs and traffic lights, we discussed school crossings and railroads, we talked about policemen and firemen and what to do if anyone ever got lost. On the playground I had the children take turns being traffic directors and helping each other across a make-believe street. This was one of the children's favorite do-and-learn activities because everybody had a role. One held the stop sign, one held the traffic lights we had made from construction paper, one wore a badge and was the policeman, and everyone crossed the street, a pretend area marked off on our section of the playground. This game worked in very nicely with our first field trip which was to the Fire Station.

I talked to the firemen at a nearby station and explained about the school, my class, and our safety studies. The men were most cooperative and more than willing to have us visit. The only reservation in my mind was about the children's reaction; would they get too excited and not follow directions. I did not mention this, however, and we went ahead with plans for our first field trip.

I need not have worried. The children were model

students, quiet, courteous, and totally attentive. The firemen showed us all around the station and explained their entire procedure from the time a call came until the fire truck left the station. They saved the best part for last. One of the men came down the pole from the second floor and landed right in front of where we were standing. The children were naturally delighted. We thanked the men and returned to class. Naturally all sixteen of my children wanted to grow up and be firemen, girls included! But the real purpose of the trip was accomplished. I wanted the children to have a personal experience with the people who guard our safety, to know for themselves that these people were their friends, that they were to be trusted and called upon if the need arose. It seemed very important to me, as two of my students came to school by bus and several more were let out and picked up in front of the school. Nearly every child would eventually mature and be trained well enough to go on errands, perhaps only to the corner store, perhaps further. Whatever the case might be, each child should know what to do in case of an emergency, what to do if he got lost, whom to trust, whom to ask for help. We studied and practiced safety the entire year.

Our next field trip was to the circus. I have already discussed the unit of work built around this trip. We prepared for it for several weeks; everything from reading, spelling, and numbers to art and constructing our own circus in class was centered around this field trip.

The tickets were donated to the school. Every child had the opportunity to go if he chose. A few of the children went with their families in the evening, but most of my group went together in car pools from the school.

I have no way of measuring the value and pleasure the children had from this trip. I do know that at the end of the year they were still talking about it, and some of them were already asking to go again the next year. To me it was an excellent lesson in recall; it was certainly more meaningful because of the extensive work we had done beforehand;

and it was a delightful experience for each of them, since some had never been to a circus. I think that travel, field trips, family outings, and do-and-see experiences are good for any child. Certainly an event with the color and magnitude of a circus in the limited world of a retarded child is a wonderful thing. It is a lesson in safety, discipline, courtesy, responsibility, and behavior. We all learn, to a certain extent, by doing. Children can be told repeatedly how to behave in public, but they need practice. What better motivation to use that which they had been taught than a trip to see the circus. The children behaved beautifully. Anyone would have been proud of them, certainly I was.

Our third major field trip was to the zoo. All of the children had been before, but it was one of their favorite places and they wanted to go again. This was another good drill in recall. It, too, was made more meaningful because of the preparation done in class. During our circus unit we had studied a great deal about animals. The field trip to the zoo was several months later, so I reviewed the things I had taught the children earlier. Then I found a story in one of the readers about the zoo. The children in that particular reader practiced the story and then read before the class.

Our number work and vocabulary centered around the coming field trip. Each child was encouraged to bring animal pictures from magazines and tell the class about the pictures. Since the children were quite limited in their knowledge, many times telling about a picture consisted only of naming the colors, pointing out the habitat — a brown and white cow in a green field — or simply taking the picture around to each classmate and saying, "See my horse." The children were benefiting even from this simple drill. They were practicing their speech, they were learning to hold a picture correctly so that it could be seen, and they were sharing something nice with each other. Our preparation for the zoo went on for almost two weeks.

62

Finally we were ready: car pools, sack lunches, snow-cone money, and a special partner for each child.

The trip was a complete success. We left school at nine and returned at one-thirty. The children were happy and very, very tired. I put some quiet music on the record player, they put their heads on their desks, and some dropped off to sleep. I cannot emphasize too much how easily these children tire. During this field trip, for example, we toured the lower level of the zoo first. We did this slowly, in the shade, pausing to discuss the animals that interested the children. I read the information from the signs on the cages. After nearly an hour I had a planned snow-cone break. We sat on shaded benches, rested, and ate our cones. By then it was eleven o'clock. Next we toured the upper level of the zoo, part of which was not shaded, so we stopped to study only the children's favorite animals. This lasted perhaps another fifty minutes. Then we had lunch, discussed the animals, birds, and snakes we had seen and thus we had our second planned rest period. After lunch there was plenty of time for a trip through the park on the miniature train. We were back at school at one-thirty. My happy little group was exhausted.

Our fourth and last field trip was another all-day excursion, this time to the park to hunt Easter eggs, picnic, and enjoy the playgrounds. We went the Monday before Easter weekend which was a three-day holiday. This holiday and the excitement of an egg hunt was marvelous motivation for an entire unit of work in all of our subjects. The children wove baskets of colored construction paper. For table decorations to take home, they drew, decorated, and colored pictures of eggs, bunnies, and crosses. Some drew pictures of their Easter clothes for Sunday School. I put new words on the board for them to draw, color, and print. Every day we listened to our Bugs Bunny record, one of their favorites. Finally Monday arrived and we all left school for the park. The children, the parents who went with us, and I all had a grand day. We played games, drank soda water, ate sandwiches, rested, and started all over again. While the children were on the playground with several parents, three volunteers and I hid eggs. In the early afternoon we gathered back at the park, counted to ten, and the egg hunt was under way. The entire day was fun. If I had to evaluate this field trip with the other three I would say it was the least educational of all but I would have to add that it was also probably the most fun. We spent a wonderful day in the park, as any large family might do and enjoyed nature, games, the egg hunt, the playground, and most of all simply being together. That is what families are for and mine was surely no different. We took a day away from school and enjoyed being happy Indians. If the truth were known, the parents and I may have had more fun than the children.

There are many holidays, local and national, throughout the year. These present teachers and families the opportunity to do fun things with children, but things which at the same time will be helpful to the child.

For instance, at Halloween I showed the children how to make masks with construction paper and string. They traced around the pattern, cut it out, made eye openings, and practiced tying them on each other. Besides the masks, I had witch patterns, pumpkins, and turkeys. All of these were good drills for dexterity plus, of course, following directions in a group situation. At Thanksgiving we made Pilgrim hats, turkeys, and cutouts of the typical Pilgrim costume. Christmas and its coming holidays held unlimited possibilities, some of which I have already mentioned: Santas, trees, the manger scene, gifts, decorations, and cards. In addition to these, plus our counting, reading, and flash card work, we sang carols in the other rooms: "Away in a Manger," "Jingle Bells," "Santa Claus Is Coming to Town," and had a three-part rhythm band. The last day before vacation we all exchanged gifts. Here I interject a very touching and personal note. I had bought each of the children a small, personal gift, brightly wrapped. After the

64

holidays we did a large amount of recall work. When the children were discussing what they had received for Christmas, one little boy who came to school by public bus said, "And a beautiful airplane that flies through the air." The plane had cost twenty-five cents at the dime store near our school.

For Washington's birthday the children made monuments from a pattern, practiced writing that special date, and learned that George Washington was the first president of the United States. Here we compared this fact to a father's being head of the family, to add a little more meaning for the children. The monuments I had the children make were an excellent, color-cut-fold drill. They were self-standing and looked very nice. As usual the children enjoyed taking them home.

Two local celebrations which the children thoroughly enjoyed were Carnival Day at school, October the fifth, and the Battle of Flowers Parade, April the twentieth, a holiday in honor of the Alamo.

Carnival Day was an on-campus festivity held in the afternoon. That morning I had films in our room for the children so that they would be rested and well able to enjoy the carnival that afternoon. There were dart games, bingo, a loop-throw and so on with prizes for everyone. The Battle of Flowers Parade was a school holiday. As this is always a lovely parade with decorated floats, various school bands, clowns, and drill teams, most of the school children and their parents attended. Many of my group went to the parade, and I used it as a basis for oral discussion and review the following Monday. Those who did not attend in person were not left out. No child should ever be ignored. We all discussed parades, horses, bands, flowers, princesses, and music. Each child was encouraged to participate. To me, this is one of the main functions of such holidays. Everyone recalls some bit of information, present or past, and shares it with his classmates.

In addition to field trips, school functions, and holidays, there is much to be gained from a simple walk around the school grounds, or the neighborhood in which one lives. My group enjoyed such walks throughout the year. I made a point of substituting these walks for play periods several times each season as the weather changed. In the fall we all collected beautiful autumn leaves and decorated our bulletin board. We discussed the birds coming south for a warmer winter. These walks were a form of science, relaxation, and physical exercise which we all enjoyed.

Another celebration which the children enjoyed and which was permitted during school was the birthday party. On these occasions I usually reserved the last hour of school. There were no gifts exchanged; I do not believe anyone could have supported more excitement than he felt already. The children printed place cards the day before. They made favors, party hats, and birthday cards. The afternoon of the party there were such games as Pin-the-Tail-on-the-Donkey, ring-toss — with a prize for each — races on the playground, and finally ice cream and cake and everyone singing Happy Birthday. These celebrations usually lasted from twelve-thirty or one until dismissal at two o'clock. The first birthday in my group was Sarah's. As her mother taught downstairs, we had a grand week planning her party. Sarah and her classmates knew about it and were eagerly anticipating it. By two o'clock that day when the parents came for their children, there was not one clean face nor hand in my class. The children all left wearing their party hats and chocolate ice cream from ear to ear. The party was far more successful, I feel certain, than anything ever given by Emily Post — and certainly a good deal more grubby.

Any situation can be meaningful, from a field trip to a birthday party in class, especially for retarded children. It is all a part of training the child to function in a normal, everyday world. For the special child, the more of our world he is exposed to, the more accustomed he becomes,

66

and the better he adjusts. He will always, however, become more excited, be more easily impressed than the normal child. After all, the world of the retarded is more limited. Thus, what a normal child accepts as standard, such as games, ice cream and cake, is for the retarded a very special occasion. It will remain so as long as he lives. His enthusiasm is boundless.

VII THERE ARE MANY things by which a child can learn. This is particularly true for the retarded child, as his world is so limited that even the simplest of drills will broaden his horizon to a certain extent. I wanted my group to learn their names, addresses, and phone numbers. Also I hoped that they would learn the numbers to ten, at least, the days of the week, months of the year, the primary colors and some others, as well as how to tell time. Numbers stumped so many of my group that I brought several decks of cards and taught the children to play poker. We all became avid gamblers — three of a kind beat a pair, eights were higher than sevens, and so on. Who could help learning numbers? It was a matter of self-defense. Very soon I could see an overall improvement in the children's workbooks as well as their board work. I must admit that I did not check the decks of cards through the office. The curriculum guide might have approved. Again it might not have. I was at the Opportunity School to teach the children, not to study the guide, which I did not have direct access to anyway. We played poker quietly and happily all year. Luckily my room was never raided during one of our games.

For some reason bingo is a more socially acceptable game

than is poker. As I had used the former in teaching I also used it with number work. This was a particular incentive after the children began to learn their numbers from eleven through twenty. There are many card games available today, even at the dime store — animals, flowers, numbers, words. These are fun games which help a child learn as well as improve his dexterity. Art and craftwork is excellent for the child with motor difficulties. Anything from outlining a cake pan to sewing-card kits which can be used with shoe-laces rather than needle and yarn are also good beginning drills for small children, retarded children, or children afflicted by cerebral palsy.

One thing that nearly all parents can afford and which can be used at home as easily as at school is the coloring book. I particularly liked those with a word or a phrase below the picture. From these books I added many new words to the flash cards the children made. "Pony," for example, appeared in many coloring books. I knew the word was used repeatedly in several of the readers. Thus, when the child came to the word later, he already knew it. I praised him highly. "Just think, Bobby, that's a new word and you read it for me perfectly."

"You want to see my picture, Teacher?"

There it was in Bobby's coloring book. It had meaning for him. He had literally colored a new word into his reading vocabulary. Learning can and should be fun.

Charades has always been one of my own favorite games, from the time I learned to play it in my teens up to my present dotage at forty. I particularly like this game for speech therapy. The way I taught the children to play was quite simple. I put easy words that the class knew well on little slips of paper. Each child drew a paper and hid it carefully from his neighbor. Then everyone took his turn acting out his word. The first one to guess the answer was the next one to act out his word. This is a good game not only for speech but also for vocabulary review — and wiggles on rainy days. Not exactly the same as charades but very similar is a riddle game called "Who Am I," or "What Am I." It, too, is played by having the students draw a piece of paper with a word on it, then describe the word. Book, for example; I have pages and pictures, I have numbers and words. What am I? This game is better for the mind, the speech, and the vocabulary than is charades. Both games are fun and beneficial, and I did not feel that when my children were playing them they were wasting their time. I do not believe in "busy work" for any student, especially the retarded. A normal child may teach himself to a certain extent. A retarded child cannot do this. Hence his time in school is very precious and must be used efficiently and effectively.

Along with poker, bingo, charades, and crafts I encouraged the children to spend a few minutes each day with puzzles. I had chairs and a large table in one corner of my room. Here I kept puzzles and a few picture books. As the children came in of a morning, they were allowed to go to the table and work on any wooden puzzle they chose. Some of these were only five pieces. Others were of cardboard and had frames. A few were the standard twenty-piece puzzles such as one finds at the dime store. The children worked and visited quietly each morning until eight forty-five. Puzzles are a good drill in visual thinking as well as an excellent exercise for dexterity. During the year I supplemented our puzzle supply several times. By the end of the year all of my children were voluntarily working with the cardboard puzzles. I was very pleased, as most of them had preferred the large wooden puzzles the past September.

All of the games I have mentioned so far have been group activities or individual work such as with coloring books and puzzles. Another of the children's favorite activities, for any subject, was the team game. I used this throughout the year for numbers, spelling, reading, and telling time. We kept score, conscientiously, and I had the winning team and their names on the board every two weeks. I chose new captains regularly. They, in turn, selected their own teams. These wonderful, shadowy children did not perform in this area as would the normal child. Ability was not the prime factor. The team members were chosen for all possible reasons. "Sarah counts good, Ann stands in line quiet, today is Mel's birthday, Shari spells better than me, Ricky picked me last time." Each member of my class was wanted and chosen for some obvious reason. It is too bad that in a normal classroom situation the desire to win usually overshadows the compassion to choose. Perhaps performance would improve if it did not. At the Opportunity School we were a family. This feeling transgressed everything else.

Puppets and dancing were two other activities all of the children enjoyed. Frances came to school one day with a new puppet. The children were delighted to watch her slip her hand inside the glove and wiggle the puppet about. It happened to be a beguiling, green alligator named Ollie. I asked my class how many of them had puppets. Only three hands went up. After discussing the subject with the class, we made another of our unanimous decisions. We all voted to make puppets during our art period. These were very simple puppets made of brown lunch bags. They were brightly colored with crayolas or water colors, as each student wished. Some of the puppets had ears either glued or stapled on, others had fancy collars of fabric. All of them were animals, so we decided to put on a puppet show. This we did and it was such fun that I had the children invite their parents to come early the next day to see their show. Many of them came. They were as delighted as I at the funny giggles and jokes at our puppet show.

Whereas the puppet project was soon over, dancing was something I taught the children one day a week after school all year. I also let them dance sometimes on rainy days when we were forced to stay indoors. I taught them about twenty minutes each week, and only then those who wanted to stay; but it is difficult to describe how much

71

my little group enjoyed their "Dancing Day." Seldom did anyone not stay for this special lesson. We began in the fall with simple dances such as "Ring-Around-the-Rosie." By spring the children had progressed through "Ten Pretty Girls" and were beginning "Skip-to-My-Lou." These dances sound so simple to us, as we read the names and recall our folk dancing in physical education class. But there is nothing simple about dancing — keeping time to the music and remembering the right steps — for a retarded child who is perhaps the equivalent age of a normal three to five year old. My children loved dancing; they worked hard at it, and although not everyone learned each dance, it was a fun, togetherness time. It was also excellent for their coordination.

I cannot say too much for television and movies, cartoons, film strips, and slides. This new dimension in education has been a blessing for all children — the poor can travel, the brilliant can watch scientific experiments, the drama student can see Shakespeare, the retarded can become better acquainted with the world in which they live. Cars, foods, animals, nature, law enforcement, music — all of these things are captured and reproduced for the viewer. As only one example of my group's interest and enrichment from television, after I began our geography classes, the children began to watch the weather forecast. We discussed snow and rain on our big map, and several of my students were even able to tell the class what the weather would be like the following day. At the Opportunity School I had access to a slide projector as well as film strips: animals, nature, flowers, fish. There were children's cartoons as well, with dialogue written in. All of the children enjoyed these and some of my better readers were even able to read the simple captions. This pleased us all.

I should mention again the benefit from such projects as our grocery store which was a truly meaningful experience. Also I want to reemphasize the importance of our field trips. Certainly this project and these trips were an important part of my children's year. There are many things to learn by. I have discussed only a few of the ones which my group particularly enjoyed. Some required extensive preparation while others did not; but each one was done with patience and praise. Learning can and should be fun, especially in a dim world that can be brightened by see-and-touch, do-and-learn, love-and-share activities.

VIII THE FORUM WAS a weekly class I began in late September. Usually on Friday afternoon we had a general discussion group about various subjects that eleven to seventeen-year-olds need to know: makeup, dress, manners, cleanliness, morals, behavior, current movies, personal experiences. As retarded children are eager to share with each other anything from cough drops to crayolas, I had no problem with class participation. Everyone wanted to contribute to the discussion; everyone did. It may seen unusual that I incorporated a class of this nature into a public school group of retarded children; but very often a child will take more seriously information taught at school rather than at home. My group at the Opportunity School needed guidance in every field possible. Some of the children came from large families in which both parents worked. One or two were only children. Several had older and younger siblings; one came to school by bus. It was for the benefit of the child, as well as his family, that I began such a class.

There is much information available to a teacher or a parent in the field of guidance. There are excellent children's magazines with articles and short stories. Besides these, school counselors have many booklets treating with special subjects. These may be borrowed, studied, and returned to the counselor. Often these booklets are a series of very brief stories about children and are followed by questions designed to stimulate class discussion: Should Sally have told the grocer when he gave her too much change? Why did Johnny enjoy picking on younger boys?

My children at the Opportunity School were particularly well groomed, they were courteous, they followed directions well, yet I began to notice little things that made me feel a guidance class once a week could be profitable.

One little girl, for instance, was prone to come to school neatly dressed but very often with dirty fingernails. There was a little boy whose hair was always combed at eight-thirty when he arrived, but by nine o'clock not one hair was in place. He obviously needed to carry a comb and to use some type of hair-grooming preparation. It seemed logical to begin with grooming.

I asked the children to bring a picture from a magazine of some boy or girl whom they thought was very nice looking — dress, suit, shoes, hair, simply a neat, nice-looking person. Luckily for me I collected these pictures as the children arrived and went through them before our discussion that afternoon. The pictures were large and colorful; all of the children or adults in them were very nice looking. Many were models wearing the latest fashions. Then I came upon a genuine jewel of a picture: a voluptuous blond, with flowing hair, standing on a cloud, and wearing a lace brassiere, matching panties, and a nylon peignoir. According to the caption on the picture she was advertising shampoo. Obviously she could not advertise the shampoo in my discussion group. Before we began that afternoon I selected five or six pictures. I had each child select two favorites and tell what he liked about each. During the discussion someone mentioned clean shoes. This was a good chance to discuss the importance of washing the face properly, using a nail brush for cleaning fingernails, and how boys and girls could comb their hair so that it would stay in place and

75

look nice. "Valentine, your hair always looks neat. Would you mind telling me how you get it to stay that way?" He was quite pleased.

"Sure, Teacher. It's some blue stuff in a jar. I think from the grocery store." My Indian with the disheveled hair spoke up.

"You copy the name for me, Valentine."

"Sure. You get some too. It smells good."

At this point everyone wanted to smell Valentine's hair. With the usual group of children this might have been embarrassing but not with these children. Valentine was quite pleased, and he was right too. The hair groom preparation smelled good.

From grooming the first week I took up dress the following week. We discussed school clothes, play clothes, Sunday School outfits, and summer and winter wearing apparel. The children enjoyed describing their favorite clothes. Sometimes we became so interested in a subject that we spent several weekly discussions on it. During October I eased the children into the area of behavior and morals which was my real purpose in starting this class. Here I used film strips on safety and manners, followed by our usual discussion. In the area of morals and behavior I found stories in children's magazines. These had good object lessons and gave us many things to discuss. In a class of retarded children, grouped by ability rather than age, the usual problems of puberty must be faced honestly, yet tactfully. What girls and boys should and should not do present quite a challenge. I could not divide us into two groups, boys and girls, because the class was accustomed to working as a family. I felt also that this would only make the older boys and girls more curious, and the younger ones might feel left out. So we stayed together as a group and simply discussed the stories I read, or the problems some of the children brought up.

For instance, one little girl was fifteen. Her sixteen-year-old sister was allowed to go to movies with her boyfriend. My little girl, though physically mature, would always be a child mentally. Certainly she could not have dates as her sister had. This was a delicate situation, especially since she was an attractive girl quite interested in boys, and they in her. I discussed the problem with her mother to be certain she knew about it. I was relieved to find out that the mother not only knew about it but also had made certain her daughter was never left alone. Rather than resenting my concern for her child, because certainly this was not any of my business, she appreciated my interest and thanked me for it. Later in the year this same mother asked for a conference after school. At this time she brought up the subject of sterilization, (chapter ten).

I may have treated our discussions on behavior a little too tactfully. I thought matters were progressing nicely. The children enjoyed our forum and certainly it was good for their speech. Each one had something to say about the various subjects we discussed. Things were going well, or so I thought. Then spring came and with it visible signs of love. I add here only one specific instance as an example of the constant care a parent of a retarded child must show.

On the first floor of our building were two rest rooms, on opposite sides of the hall, the only one available to our students. Seated beside the girls' room, in the hall, there was always our friend, Cora. I sometimes thought she was literally glued to her chair. Occasionally she would enter the rest room to help one of the girls or boys. She was an elderly Negro lady of vast patience and understanding — probably more than we six teachers put together. Each class had its special break at which time we accompanied the students to the rest rooms and waited in the hall. One spring day Cora appeared at my door with one of my little girls by the hand. She had been excused during class.

"You better watch this one. She has a friend in Mrs. Allen's room."

Cora, alert as usual, had discovered the girl inside the rest room holding hands with a boy from Mrs. Allen's room.

How the two children got behind the door in the girls' room, Cora and I will never understand. Luckily some little girl called out to Cora for assistance, and the boy and girl had been discovered. They were blissfully standing behind the main entrance holding hands. Yes, love had bloomed. Cora and I tried to curtail Cupid all spring.

The principal benefits from my forum-type class once a week were perhaps few but valid. To begin with, it was excellent speech therapy. Every one of my children wanted to contribute an opinion, an idea, a phrase. These were spontaneous reactions and so delighted me more. After all, life is give and take, question and answer, communication. My children were learning this. Secondly, I felt that through our discussions the children were learning to adjust to commonplace situations. I was not reading them fairy tales during this period each week but rather samples from our natural world, our everyday life. Thirdly, my children were learning tolerance through understanding — the little boy who was hungry at home and took an apple from the grocery store was not the same little boy who swiped bubble gum at the drug store just to see if he could get away with it.

Probably the most delightful comment made by any of my children came during one of our forum discussions. Here I recall another quotation of which I am very fond, "Out of the mouths of babes . . ." This particular day we were having a very serious discussion about a little boy in a story who was a terrible behavior problem at school. Yet the same boy went home each day, helped around the house, and even set the table in the evening for his mother. The discussion question was quite clear: what could his problem be? Jimmy's hand went up at once.

"He's maladjusted, Teacher. He needs to see an analyst."

Jimmy was probably right, but at this point I felt that perhaps the boy and I both needed to see one. To say the least, our forum was very interesting all year.

IX WERE I to let myself, I know I could write an entire book on our school play. The mere idea of sixteen retarded children memorizing lines and performing on a stage still leaves me in awe; at the same time it seemed perfectly natural. The fact that they made their own costumes in class under my supervision — I have never believed in homework, and most assuredly not for parents — only added to my pride and their self-importance.

It seemed that late each spring it was customary for each group in the Opportunity School to put on one P.T.A. program together. This year it came on March the twenty-first. One group sang and used rhythm instruments, another group clapped to nursery tunes, still another did folk dancing. As my class had particularly enjoyed several story records over a period of months, I asked the children how they would like to put on a play. I had my usual one hundred-percent cooperation. Everyone raised his hand in favor of this idea.

Now that we had decided on our part for the P.T.A. program, we had to decide what play to give. Since the past fall my class had enjoyed five excellent story records. In fact the children had listened to them so often that they frequently quoted various lines as the record was playing, pronouncing words they could neither read nor spell, and doing this very nicely. It occurred to me that from one of these familiar story records we could select our play.

The children and I talked about each story and decided upon "Robinhood." There were plenty of parts for everyone, plus four major roles and a lot of action.

This having been decided, I began to play the record once every day asking the children to pay very close attention to all of the parts. I explained about tryouts and let each child decide which person he would rather be: Robinhood, the Sheriff of Nottingham, Little John, Maid Marian, one of the Merrymen of Sherwood Forest, or the stage manager, or the prop man. Naturally several children wanted to be each character. We listened to the record and discussed the parts all week. I told the children that the only way to be fair was for each one to try out for the part he liked, and then the class would vote. This way we would have the best person for each part and our play would be a grand success. Everyone would have an important part, be a star. We had our tryouts for several afternoons. Each one of the children was voted to play a particular part. Then we began rehearsal. It was March the first. Our P.T.A. program was the twenty-first. That meant we had about sixteen school days and only thirty minutes a day of each. Our studies had to continue as usual. Here I relied heavily on repetition. Each child had heard the record from which his lines were taken so many times that the material should be as an old friend, familiar and comfortable. To be certain, I copied the lines and let each student take home his few sentences. I explained that this was to help his parents, "just in case they want to hear your lines before the play." I made certain these little dialogues were not sent home until the week of the program — no homework for parents. By that time, of course, the children knew their parts very well and were quoting our record almost verbatim.

During these sixteen days of rehearsal our artwork was centered around the costumes for the play. Depending upon the part, each student made a hat, or bow and arrows. These were made from newspapers folded a certain way, and from sapling branches peeled to the core and tied with string. Each had to be painted an appropriate color with tempra paints. The rest of the costume was composed of blue jeans and a shirt, the usual apparel for school boys. Only one slight problem remained: Frances was elected to be the Sheriff of Nottingham. This problem was overcome when she told me her brother's jeans and shirt "fitted good." Maid Marian had a nice Sunday School choir robe, so our costumes were ready.

I discussed makeup with the children. I carefully explained to the boys that their faces had to be slightly darkened too, so that they would not "look like milk and all white" under the lights. Bless their hearts; they may not have understood, but each child eagerly agreed to let me put on his makeup for the play. Our last and funniest experience was keeping Little John's stomach in place. The pillow simply refused to stay put. We finally conquered this matter with large safety pins as well as a belt, and we were ready for our one dress rehearsal, the day before the program.

I suppose from Broadway to the elementary school play, drama is always plagued by crisis. Our production was surely no exception. March the twentieth came. One o'clock. It was time for our dress rehearsal. We went to the cafeteria-auditorium to practice. My prop man had everything ready behind the curtains. Our stage manager had everyone lined up according to his part — as we were a family, he could do this easily by first names. Everyone was in his place. Our prop man pulled the curtains and "Robinhood" began. In a short time Maid Marian appeared. I could hardly hear her, and I was sitting in the third row from the stage. Suddenly she looked peculiar. She barely turned her head from side to side, her neck was thick and puffy. Heaven

81

help us — Sarah had the mumps! The school nurse confirmed my worse suspicions, and Maid Marian went home, not to return for eight days. This trauma presented a slight problem, especially since the P.T.A. program was the next night. I quickly drafted my shy, little Sherry whose voice was weak but whose gestures were fine, in addition to which she could wear Sarah's choir robe, and she knew all the lines. James Cohen, Napoleon, nor Alfred the Great ever plotted faster. Rehearsal continued. "Robinhood" seemed in fine form for the P.T.A. We ran through it quickly one more time; Sherry's voice seemed louder, and we were back in our room for some reading drills before two o'clock dismissal. The costumes were carefully put in the cloakroom, and all of the children went home happy. They were ready for their play the following evening. Each one had been individually praised; the stage manager and the prop men had been profusely thanked. Everyone was completely indispensable.

The next day I omitted practice. I played our story record only once for fun. The children chimed in with the dialogue if they so chose. Aside from our regular studies I planned a relaxed day. Retarded children cannot and should not be pressured. Before dismissal I mentioned the play that evening only to the extent that we had prepared a lovely surprise for Mommy and Daddy, Brother and Sister, Aunt and Uncle — the entire family was welcomed. The school, of course, had sent home invitations for the special P.T.A. entertainment.

I cannot start to describe our play that night. Only a beginning teacher, or one with many years of experience, would undertake such a project. "Robinhood" was next to the last presentation on the program, I think perhaps because my group was considered educable. We were followed by folk dancing and the coffee hour. (By March I truly feel that I had conscienteously worked my way into such disfavor that we were on the program simply because each room had to participate and the parents were present.) I

82

clearly recall that my principal came forward with a benevolent smile to announce that my room would present a play. There was a note of gentle, nauseating patience in her voice. She sat down. I dimmed the lights and the play began.

For twelve, solid, fun-packed minutes my happy tribe of Indians dashed, darted, fell, shot arrows, and shouted lines at each other across the stage. The audience was completely quiet. I did not hear even one cough — man, woman or child — and when the lights came up and the curtain closed there was complete silence. Then suddenly the entire auditorium was standing and clapping wildly; some were actually crying. Others were laughing with delight and perhaps relief. These parents were certainly not all from my room. There were five other rooms, some with as many children as I had in my group. Later I realized why the response. It had been a note of hope, a moment of joy, a future triumph for the younger children. The applause continued. Finally Miss Smith came forward again, this time to announce the folk dancing.

At the coffee hour after the program I was engulfed by parents, most of whom I did not know. This did not matter; they were part of the Opportunity School family. We all worked together. I answered their questions as best I could. Their children had given the play. I had only worked the lights backstage. My incredible, happy Indians had presented "Robinhood." I was tired that night when I got home, but so terribly content. My group had been a great success. If I could sense this, surely my children could feel it too. It was very warm and comfortable being wanted and appreciated.

The next day Miss Smith came to my room and asked me to bring my class to the auditorium to put on our play again. One of the fathers in another room did a great deal of work in his spare time on behalf of mental retardation. He wanted to film our play. I explained to my children that a special friend wanted a movie of "Robinhood." The children were delighted and gladly performed again with great enthusiasm. Somewhere, even today, my children are on film. This delights me, as the thought of our helping even one depressed parent is worth the effort. It was not really so much after all. It was a fun project incorporating recall, repetition, and craftwork. To me, coupled with the reactions of the parents, it was the personification of the quotation which begins, "Hope springs eternal . . ."

X I HAVE TRIED to put into words a few of my experiences in this other world, the one in which I was privileged to enter and dwell for nine months. My words are inadequate to express the many moods and varied feelings I had. The fact that the children let me enter, shared their emotions, and made me a part of their own particular twilight zone was more than a reward. It was a pleasure, a privilege, and is now a rare memory to be treasured always. Perhaps, too, it was a touch of destiny. As I have said, I was not a patient person, nor am I yet to an extremity; but today when I discover a slow learner in my regular class, what I used to try to overcome with discipline, I now try to persuade with understanding and in some cases with a maternal affection and gentle guidance I did not have. I know that I learned more from my group at the Opportunity School than they learned from me. This knowledge I shall use always.

It seems that many people in our world today have some grievous complaint to make, a reason for carrying banners and raising loud voices in protest. I cannot do anything about such actions as a teacher in a public school system except try to pass on to my classes the lessons I learned at the school for the mentally retarded: patience, praise, love,

85

recognition, importance. Armed with these credos, I do not see how anyone can fail to succeed in his own way, at his own rate.

My one regret, and my principal reason for recounting my experiences, is that there are still parents and people in the world who feel confusion and even shame at seeing or having a retarded child. Here, in my thinking, always comes to mind one of my favorite quotations: "Suffer the little children to come unto me. For theirs is the kingdom of heaven."

What little children? The brilliant, the beautiful, the Hebrew? Not one word was said of this, only, "theirs is the kingdom of heaven." Perhaps my happy group who loved and shared so willingly were already partly there. I know only that they showed me the way into another world, the one in which such axioms as "Love thy neighbor," and "Do unto others" were the unwritten law, the instinctive sentiment. For this I shall always be grateful.

Why does one go into special education for the handicapped, or the retarded? My personal reason was very simple. I had hoped to become a doctor at one point in my growing up. Also during this time I discovered that the minister at my church, whom we all greatly admired — a man of deep, human compassion — had a retarded son, a mongoloid. I seldom saw the boy, even in my adult years, because he had a cardiac condition which prevented his attending the Opportunity School or going out much. Thus I wanted to know more about the field of special education. Fortunately while at the university I was lucky enough to study under a Dr. Wolff. During this too-brief course one summer, his class ran the gamut from the very talented, to the handicapped, to the mentally retarded. Those of us who chose to do so, volunteered at the Cerebral Palsy Center in town. This proved to be an invaluable experience for me later at the Opportunity School when I began to teach some of my group to button their coats and tie their shoes. The students

86

at the Cerebral Palsy Center were not retarded; they were afflicted. But they had the same problems as some of my group. Neither could perform a certain, routine function, dressing himself. One problem was physical, the other mental.

The means to conquering this problem was the same: practice, repetition, dexterity. Whatever one chooses to call it, this can be overcome in nearly every instance with patience, love, praise, and practice. Mental retardation is neither a sin nor a crime. It is a circumstance of our world. It can be met, understood, and helped to a certain degree. There is always hope, for those with us now, and for those to come. The sooner a neighbor learns to walk into the home of his friend where a twelve-year-old is playing with blocks on the floor and say, "Hi, Johnny. Gee those are pretty blocks," the better the child, the parent, and the friend will feel. There is absolutely no need for shame. There is a need, however, for friendship and understanding.

One question which I was asked several times during my year at the Opportunity School concerned sterilization. As my group ranged in age from eleven to sixteen, several of the parents had children reaching puberty. My only answer to this question was on an individual basis according to the type retardation and the intelligence level of the student. Most parents of normal children would do anything to protect, comfort, and help their children. Parents of retarded children are surely not any different; but added to their usual responsibilities is the fact that they have a special child to provide and care for, one who will need supervision as long as he lives. Physically he will mature. Mentally he will not. So, as a means of protecting a retarded child from harming or being harmed, I can see nothing wrong with sterilization. Certainly I would consult an authority, a doctor, and perhaps a minister before deciding on this measure. In some cases retarded children are born sterile, in other instances they are not. I could only listen to the parents who came to see me about this problem, then advise that the decision be made with the child, his future, and the family in mind.

Children should bind a family together, not create a schism. Of all the parents I have ever known I have never seen closer cooperation than with parents of retarded children. They were totally and completely together with me, with their children, and with the other parents at the Opportunity School. They had put behind them the competition one often sees in a regular school situation. They had become a working unit, each proud and pleased at every child's accomplishment. They were a delight to work with. There was no shame, no reticence, only an attitude of "What can I do?" They were truly marvelous people.

I suppose nearly any teacher, regardless of his field, could write pages on curriculum and texts versus experience. Certainly there are two sides to any question; but I personally have never found anything in a book so valuable as is the actual doing, seeing, and being experience. I do not believe any number of books could ever have taught me the things I learned at the Opportunity School. Warmth, love, kindness, tenderness do not come from pages in a book. They come from people. In my case they came from very special children who blindly trusted me to lead them. Having been in this position I can only say one tries harder. Here I pause to add a very personal though not bitter, perhaps disappointed is a better word, view point. I do not think it fair that anyone in a supervisory position, such as was my principal, be called upon to perform a task for which he is not prepared. Miss Smith had been assigned the job of principal of the Opportunity School in addition to her regular job as principal of the adjoining elementary school. For the latter she was, to me, highly qualified. She was an experienced elementary school teacher who later became a principal.

She was an excellent disciplinarian; but she had never spent one full day in a room with sixteen retarded children, much less one entire year. Yes, she had taken courses in this field to improve her understanding. She was conscientious, willing, and intelligent. She was totally inexperienced. It was a major breakthrough when I was allowed to teach my educable group to tell time. It was beyond reason that they be taught any form of geography. This was not in the curriculum. At this point I felt like shouting "Oh, nuts!" But there they were: Nicky, Sarah, Bobby, Felipe — a shy smile, a tug on the sleeve. Who could refuse these precious children? The curriculum be damned. We would have a good year anyway. And we did.

One major factor in contributing to the success of our year was the parents. There is shame, dismay, pity, scorn, and a definite desire not to discuss the subject of retarded children among many people. Fortunately these attitudes are disappearing, gradually. Among my parents I was not confronted with any of these Old Wives' views. Once a parent has faced the fact that his child is retarded and sets about to help that child in the best way he can, half the battle is won. He becomes a member of a team, but a very unusual team in which each player is alike to a certain degree. Once over this barrier and having entered his child in an Opportunity School, the parents soon realized that here is the right thing for the child. We all need to progress and succeed at our own rate. The retarded child is certainly no different in this respect. He needs recognition, achievement, and understanding. The fact that his progress is slower than that of the normal child is all the more reason for entering him in special education. He desperately needs to be with his own kind. He needs his own world of individual attention, love, kindness, and patience.

It is no wonder that the children at the Opportunity School adored Monday through Friday. They were with their kind, working on their level, being praised and encouraged as they were being trained. At the end of the school year the parents of each child received a suggestion sheet for summer training. Thus the habits of the past year could be continued and stressed at home. (Figure 8, pages 90-91)

SUGGESTIONS FOR SUMMER TRAINING –
AUSTIN OPPORTUNITY SCHOOL

I *Behavior*

1. Be sure that they say, "Good Morning" and "Good-Bye" when it is appropriate.
    Also have them say, "Come in and sit down" whenever possible when friends arrive.
    Have them say, "Excuse me," "Please" and "Thank you" when necessary.

2. Be sure that they use only their own possessions such as combs, brushes, toothbrushes, etc. See that they are willing to share their toys with others but be sure that their things are returned to the rightful owner since children must be trained to keep and take care of their own things and let the other child have what is his.

3. Be sure that they have opportunities to be with other children.
    They all need to continue contacts with others of their own ages.

4. Give each one his own simple responsibilities and see that they accept them. Children enjoy knowing that certain things are their own duties and they gain in confidence, ability and a sense of security through having them.

II *Health Habits*

1. See that they care for their teeth in the morning and at night.

2. Train them to file and clean their nails.

3. Check on their toilet habits and keep them regular.

4. Compliment them on personal appearance and keep them interested in the bath, clean clothes and neat hair.

5. Watch posture and compliment them for walking, standing and sitting correctly.

6. Give opportunities for exercise — ball games, swimming, walking, simple calisthenics, games of different kinds with other children if possible.

7. Keep them interested in normal weight. Weigh often.

III *Academic Education*

1. Give drills in telling: name, age, birthday, and address. The older ones can give telephone numbers.

2. Drill on telling names of the days. The older children could give the month and date.

3. Counting is good. With the small children count objects only.
They must see and handle what they are counting. The older children may do simple addition where the sum is not more than 10.

4. Do not *push* the child in anything. Make all drills *fun*.

Do not forget that the child has lost the companionship of his fellows in school so give him all the love and attention possible to make up for the letdown of having nowhere to go.

Figure 8

In completing this story of my year at the Opportunity School I have a great desire to leave the parents, relatives, teachers, and friends of these special children with some message, some profound words, something to cling to for those who feel terribly discouraged. Although the desire is present, the words are not. I recall this one year in my life not with tears but rather with a smile and a feeling of nostalgia. Surely this was my most rewarding experience. Thus selfishly I conclude this story. The many memories of nine wonderful months are mine forever. I am deeply grateful to these special children who let me enter and share their world of fantasy and affection, of kindness and trust, of joy and love — their world and mine, for a time, of Cotton Candy and Carrousels.

Carrousels

Is half enough?
Round and round,
Up and down.
Parents praise,
Children wave.
Round and round,
Up and down.
Faces pale,
Outsiders fail.
Round and round,
Up and down.
Winds blow cold,
Parents grow old.
Round and round,
Up and down —
A hope to hide,
A dream to ride!
Round and round,
Up and down.
Is half enough?